Once again, Thilleman takes into his own writing body the chaos of the great question at its fundamental arc: who are we?—a quest that can only be pursued initially in language. He finds that language born in the mysteries of the primal urgency of our need—not so much to speak—as to think. Then, he establishes, Blake-like—a language not grammatical or ordinary, not a language merely of thinking, but a primal language rooted in the poetic of his own body, and thus this universal body we all share with this earth. Every age demands its own mythos. Thilleman creates a thoroughly contemporary mythology of consciousness which names the unnameables so that they might carry us from "Descent" all the way through chaos upon chaos, morass and vision to "what is to be known now."

Martin Nakell

song's the new being          written on her zone?

T Thilleman goes where he has to go and knows what to do when he gets there. And, when do is possible, he can. There is no poem anything like this poem anywhere near this poem—this must be the poem.

Larry Kearney

T Thilleman's thought-provoking poetic experiments challenge the mind & eye and illuminate the deepest crevices of our origins and longings, the ancient yet present and unchanging bedrock of human experience. His work deserves to be encountered, and reckoned with.

Eric Hoffman

"Become one with the sway"—TT urges us: "zone's zoom." Figures herein are some sort of psycho-somatic procedure or experiment. Logic in which "flow's polemic" is capable of discernment. The bridge made of bioluminescent threads or of fallen hairs collected from the first ape as she holds her offspring. I feel comfortable reading this book as a sacred text (Zohar), as personal manifesto or anti-memoir—as what I wish was the interior life of *Us* weekly magazine in the grocery store line—to peruse or ponder while the person in line ahead of me is looking at their cell phone and not at the grocery clerk.

j/j hastain

It is difficult, perhaps the work of a lifetime, to pin down the method, so the work then becomes the attempt. "There is an attempt to regulate the irrational aspects. So my work is always uncertain, but at the same time the uncertainty is arrested where the system breaks down, or where the incapacity comes in. To locate that is even more interesting than a willful, logical position; anybody can do that." R. Smithson, "Pointless Vanishing Points." Thilleman working to determine a method for this kind of inquiry constitutes a Williamsesque quest in Amerikan poetry so big only Olson took it on: once established, the idea is, the writer can return at will to pick up there, at the point left off, as if opening a book to the manuscript page marked, and proceed in the work. I would venture to summarize Thilleman's methodology by use of Smithson's observation that "where the system breaks down ... is ... more interesting." This is the advance Thilleman makes.

Rich Blevins

T Thilleman's *Anatomical Sketches* is a stunning display of visionary daring, formal virtuosity, and intrepid intellect engaged in a process of world discovery, where discovery is understood as an act of imagination and articulation. The two teachers who come to mind in relation to Thilleman's extensive work are Blake and Yeats. Like them he creates and populates a world of dynamic forms that range from emerging humans, to vast interstellar formations, to mythological forces, to the details of genetic exfoliation. At the heart of his committed pursuit, is the question, "What is this child of the world / Gathering sense within his wave-like singing?" This book is unique in a world of contemporary poetry dominated by precious lyrics and "avant-garde" word dumps. It takes up poetry's ancient responsibility to preserve the world by informing it. What an extraordinary accomplishment.

Michael Boughn

Thilleman's poems are playful and intellectual—a mirror of all the synapses, misfirings and disconnects that take place during the process of juggling two or three or more thoughts in the air at one time. It would be easy to say he is simply the latest offspring of a modernist/post-modernist tradition that began with Stein and Pound and continued up through Olson and Duncan, a tradition that encouraged getting lost as the way to discovering the hidden meaning of anything but Thilleman's modus operandi is impossible to pin down, a surviving force amid the endless detritus and debris of the past who happens to be alive at this peculiar all-or-nothing moment.

Lewis Warsh

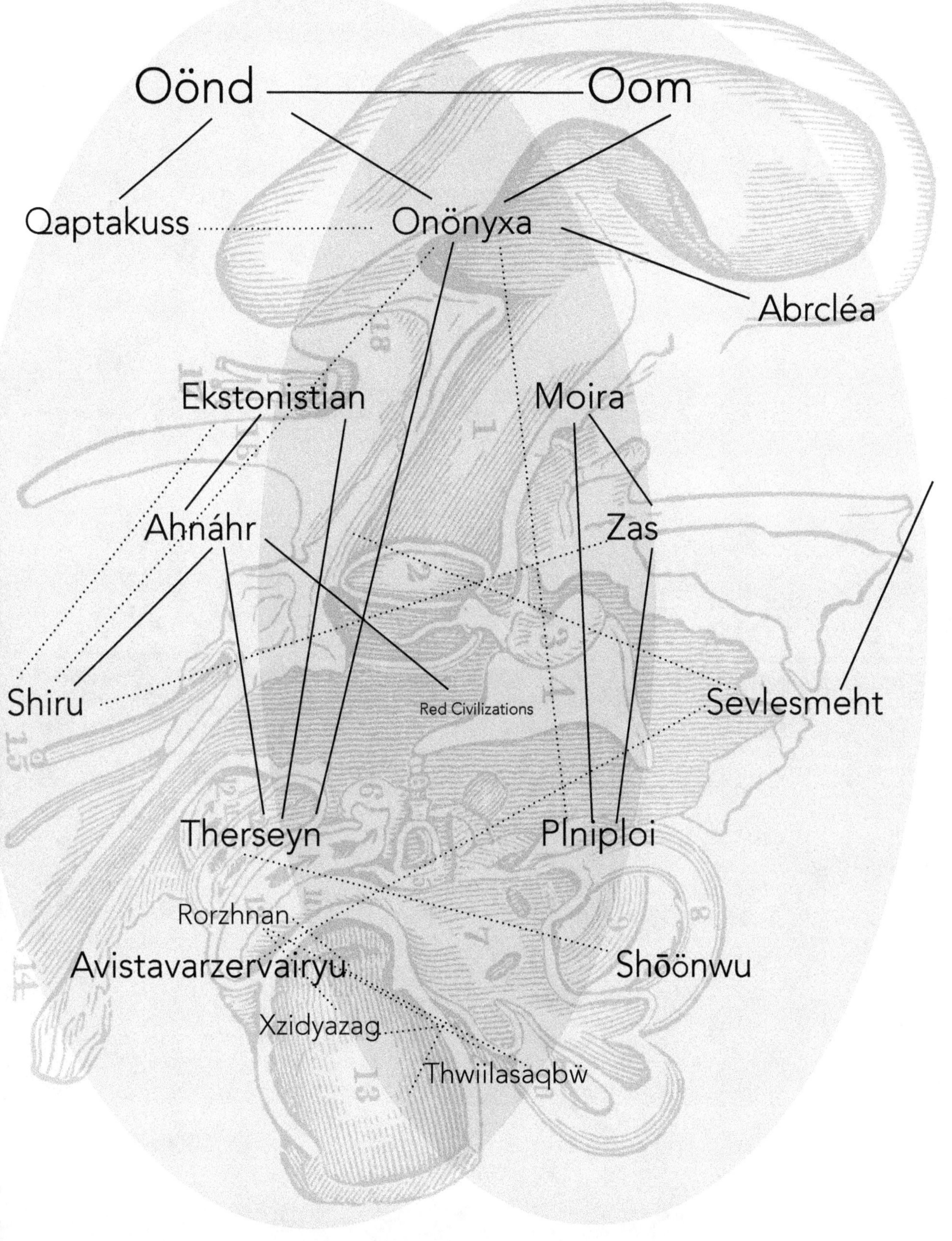

Oönd
Oom
Qaptakuss
Onönyxa
Abrcléa
Ekstonistian
Moira
Ahnáhr
Zas
Shiru
Red Civilizations
Sevlesmeht
Therseyn
Plniploi
Rorzhnan
Avistavarzervairyu
Shōōnwu
Xzidyazag
Thwiilasaqbẅ

# Descent

## t thilleman

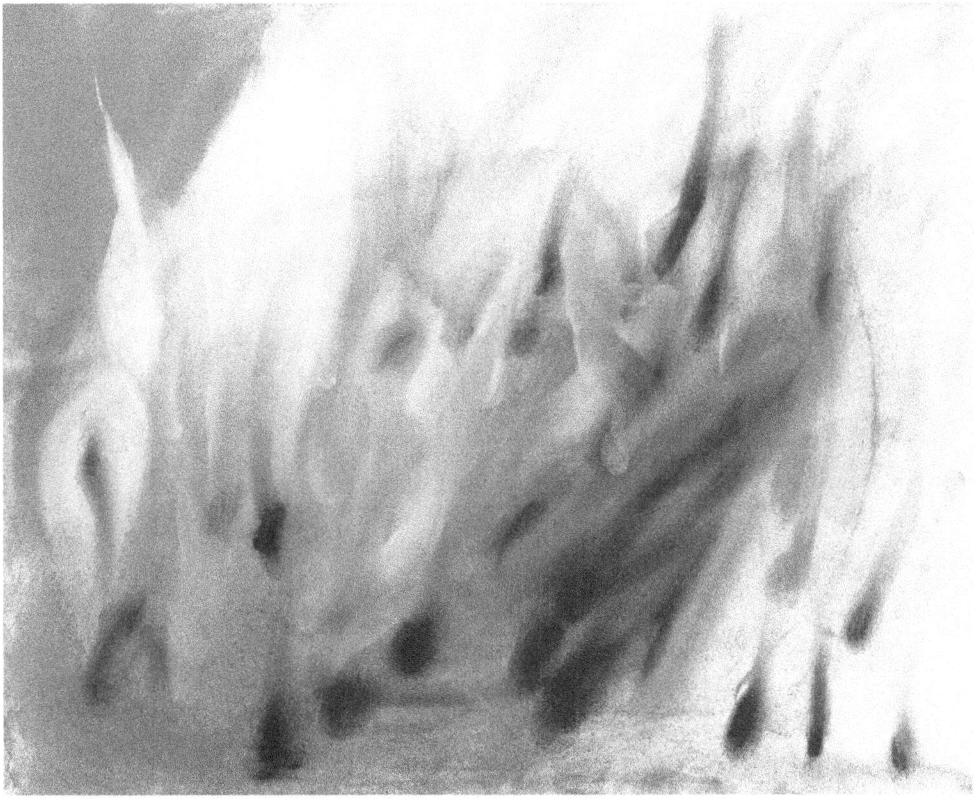

Mad Hat Press
Asheville, North Carolina

MadHat Press
MadHat Incorporated
PO Box 8364, Asheville, NC 28814



The Library of Congress has assigned
this edition a Control Number of
2018960636

ISBN 978-1-941196-80-9 (paperback)

www.madhat-press.com

First Printing

# Descent

Onönyxa & Therseyn

Norse & Forra

Sevlesmeht & the Birds

Oom & Onönyxa

*sketches, the nature of*

# Onönyxa & Therseyn

*"a 26,000 year flight awakes El Niño into La Niña    West ➔ East"*

# Anatomical Sketches

"'The lessons of the Neander Valley are not over yet,' says Stringer."
*The Observer* (1999)

"It is even likely that Neandertals had similar but less developed language abilities. (It has been said that the Neandertal larynx was not long enough to produce our richness of vowels, but there is not yet enough evidence to support such a statement.)"
Luigi Luca Cavalli-Sforza, *Genes, Peoples, and Languages* (2000)

"However, these important anatomical considerations have limited consequences for the ability of Neandertals to contrast vowels *i a u*. Our simulations show that the maximal vowel space of a given vocal tract does not depend on the larynx height index: gestures of the tongue body (and lips and jaw) allow compensation for differences in the ratio between the dimensions of the oral cavity and pharynx."
Boë et al, *Journal of Phonetics* (2002)

"The alternative is to conclude that the human capacity was born in potential by some "keystone" acquisition at or close to the birth of our species as an anatomical entity. This innovation then lay fallow, as an *exaptation*, until it was activated by some kind of behavioral invention in a particular local population. And, if that invention was highly advantageous, it's reasonable to expect that it would have spread rapidly by cultural contact among anatomically modern human populations, all over the Old World, that would already have possessed the biological potential to acquire it."
Tattersall & Schwartz, *Extinct Humans*

# Homo (erectus et alia)

call it
anatomical sketches
new look into old work investigation as scale reader into time
blinded by sight or given sight in a blinding gestation discovers not so much a land-bridge but more a **zone** re-emergence
latent genetic material
pooling our own and not our own currents of the zone the property of the pregnancy

physical dimension of the analogical spell
tells
allegorical cinema
pretend position of a peopled person history arbitrary birthplace
dwindling access to resource there their
bodies ignorant in ambulating would or will know by the zone she carries in time

being there (extinct to us in all scales) beings *here* (crowd-starved by the scale of conscious thought)

sketching the possible *pharmikon* of *mousterian* tools or any in a lithic scatter corresponds to the molecular she carries into the term of the zone
writing dendritic root-balled source initialized the contact encapsulates the small unseen size correlated eggs drift by the nature of a species whose codes inform our sperm-filled balls

digs to the center the site
penetrates networks an electrical discovery

straight thru unseen seeds no longer following order strikes into dirty loess erects a universe the zone slowly acquires by

## Clade or tree

this sketching is a place might have continued into the present or "next"
discovery of cladistic taxa      enjambment
    diagram or tree displays      lineage organisms
  attendant various studies evolve      together   "tree"
      upon which   forms live

                the term   *Clade*   Greek in ancient meaning    branching
κλάδος   splits
                  fissures or caesurae   seeds

striking

new ground's identity

trees
extinct to the      place of classification     mind's
     divergence    singular    cladicisms' taxonomy follows

uttering      yawning      abyss

zone's zoom

accidental individuation composes

two halves of one circle     wheels symbolic
splits the re

joints complete finishing     into the other

branch

survives both

by

# Processing the World-Tree

## Part 1

*the work to dissolve*

Gerrit Lansing, "The Soluble Forest"

# EKSTONISTIAN

**hid the skull waits for birth** in dirt the Daughters work and as extension homage EKSTONISTIAN chatters they finger the very edges of the wet so work and play alliance and allegiance OKEANOS rolls in a ball from the wool from the herds of waves in and out sending a fleece *so see* they say to each *see this wavy bigness begins replace even a sheepish herd we've drawn the many seeming arbitrary so the work by time and in time and so over all time*

AHNÁHR tempts hounds those empty realities who've found a sudden appearance within the world at the edge of the known before the great god OKEANOS from that and those along its very rim the nature of which blind in newness these bounds the hounds have only come from seeming stellar reaches for the deep the ocean is as of space but the unknown of a deepening both now's a Plain where wild beasts in infinite shape but from one shape evolved to hunt and the hunt for the one woman the hunting ritual the world over the hunted knows so creates a copse or small wood

in the Forest news of the dead head told the FAERY protected sanctity the green grove yet with majesty with power of flight the fair the animal Forest a strength a practice in the pleasure of Earth strode golden yin-yang means thru its FAERYLAND setting all within to disburthen and thus burthen gathering sweat the ringing even-tones above and ye also equal by all nations a synapse of Flowers a seduction of love-lorn space in time of the end the temporal winding way the plant-life the space time mankind in early days the dawn of THERSEYN's inner ear his jaw in a rut as if rotten

ZAS and MOIRA even AHNÁHR who has a rumor within still permutated by the waves of OKEANOS the Ocean the surround sound amphitheatrical inter-independent telluric chitter-chatter each distaff staged casts we-aves running the floor of the world the stage then a sparkling golden shaft or spool erect such energetic play ZAS an emblem in other words on the tattoo-side of the skin in such places or the land as it too trails and paths trails and smelling salts trace his gaseous length

OKEANOS the Earth and all who witness swear to the seasonal roundness satisfied ready to conclude    *look at the rain the snow the sun the wind ergo this that the other and the mother too well it must be MOIRA who's shot so we take a sign the embodiment or stolid factotum the actual employee the model citizen the very library our every essence thus from her*

AHNÁHR resounds from the Forest EKSTONISTIAN has been put or fled in disgust and yet full that God wanting her distance again so reminded there of MOIRA by FAERY presences organic substance atomically round empty *and* full proton electron grace resounds torrential the RED CIVILIZATIONS whose historical mission re-ignites under vaporous shades of ZAS and MOIRA in atmosphere the Stage and the State in nothing more persuasive nor evasive nor penetrating than the gaseous to hold strong together reasoning contention continuously conflating for which EKSTONISTIAN receives more terminal blame her hair on fire now in gaseous aether of Earth her dendritic abode the grove the Forest of Earth central

stealing the breath of the world thru Stages of Man hard and swift final completely out of the world never to return never re-cycle discarded carbons defining Law barren hollow a pure curse now think the definition of MOIRA truth and tested Law everything which bore reality reason into this present you will see the program SEVLESMEHT works in fire to make smoke of image thus force the world toward vision any vision comprised of smoke any visage there retains temporal might of the world binding men toward sight

yet what quiet and still power rules the stars binds AHNÁHR's robes in milk-white light a-vault the heaven of extreme emptiness where Earth below inhales being to come by sweet space the quenching air of summer cold abandonment winter's uninhabitable mountain ranges the brooding vast call circulates now to AHNÁHR to centers of dim Man Woman tidal OKEANOS the edge of knowledge hushes all proceedings over-arches the peremptorily ridiculous vision-quest of SEVLESMEHT so the Daughters of OKEANOS pass to AHNÁHR then onto ZAS around the world til symmetry's achieved the center of the asymmetrical it is to the work of the Daughters from generation to generation rough walls the edge of Earth the holes spumey oceanic eruptions

AHNÁHR is lives sees conquers so Stages give way to States clamping the skull into place begins a war with the gaseous god begins also a way of no return a way of searching the past within the present

*what you've planned yes planned what you've wrought yes wrought by those tails of clouds in aetherial soup come to take these waves and the Daughters in the weaving forms in almost random excess upon oxygen's universal reaches the edge of galaxies with the tyranny of abandoned evacuations   this kind of obedience not simply outward but limp ZAS   channel his erections away from the Earth   out this endless ZAS-work it's really freaking unreal   it's really just a frozen ark of images stills symbolic resonance will drown in what it was four and a half billion years ago … … …*

each soul moves to this State from Stages of Man evolution happens mingling an order destined from the space of red-hot vermillion-clouded endless interstices the black ages the place of Earth a ZAS-borne age the morphologies of mind body lung and heart all distances all the widening engulfing calling names of deceased a blast of thunder the atmosphere the lightning cracking across immense space resounds AHNÁHR's realm the weather an overlap a place where Earth where the Old the New meet and seem to become one another

the RED CIVILIZATIONS think ZAS others AHNÁHR whom they remember so within and without the human fold the humming vitalic tidal wave of sound carries news whether intercepted by rods or shafts or waves of ZAS smoky televisories of SEVLESMEHT or let loose toward never-ending distances the breathing now capacitated Daughters some fainting unable to recover what the brain told the fingers perform thus all memory becomes ancient and mimetically stands for sight

the RED CIVILIZATIONS attempting from the shaman SEVLESMEHT seem as temporal evolutionary and so all doubles and trebles into the swelling cranium the world whirling in magnetic polarities of Stage and State planet to planet star to star galactic dust ZAS might muster or AHNÁHR swear now anew comes to precessional activity

AHNÁHR not deterred presses toward this world lays his creation EKSTONISTIAN to the Forest floor into her front goes all the major Daemon's prowess   *ah the sweet Earth*   he says and at last he's able to completely show completely fall toward this Earth this time this New World the front of her forehead's mound entirely reflected a pool impressed of the underside the Grove's canopy a scroll or leaf wood-fiber reflective capacity the beginning of time itself imprinted symbolic New World this moment ushers   *ah ah ahnnnnnn*

EKSTONISTIAN understands the universal and not her one captivity in knowledge of time but time she holds in evolving nature captivated by the deep well of calculated time calculated value symbolic tones surrender hiding leaving human incapacitated illiterate and the nations enter a Stage of World-Time reason has thrown to the dogs hunting gaming mauling as it should be

SEVLESMEHT everything within and without commences too the world become subordinate to the holy blind consumption blind waste symbolic relation to own them master them so somehow the world must be unmasked but this is what is waiting within without the very universality particularized procreation the industrious act AHNÁHR imprinted upon EKSTONISTIAN

SEVLESMEHT rounds up encampments of RED CIVILIZATIONS and calls their chieftains psychopomps and shows the fingers on his hand says

*there are 4 ages I mean 5 ages skip that I mean to say there are 5 ages*   and he holds up his hand and shows it to all of them it is as if he's just seen his hand for the first time   *known to us from the beginning the Earth and each of them measured I received transmission not too long ago they have names these five they are … … … … …   wait   … … … … …   wait for it wait   … … … … …*

SEVLESMEHT's tent in the vast desert of the world the small limbs of wood the pupil-dark bitumin given only to its burning for the reading of what now flaunting into face the universal atomic law a fossilized schizophrenia they call politics even in small stretches of the insect larvae the same appraisal of slug gleaming slime on rocks and dirt the moon shines off its trail

AHNÁHR has come to undo sufferers undo all material connection by his half-life entrance to this world knowledge of radioactivity all matter shows meeting death in life and vice versa to undo the free from non-suffering for he is the Law of all half-life his robes are white in the wind of this world and they rule from creation time *and* space Man *and* God *and* EKSTONISTIAN

Law made universal fucking!

productive engines mine the Earth for fossil moralizing fuel flatulent the Air in signs of smog conducting SEVLESMEHT's tele-visory does not understand designs of these two ZAS now his other marbleized and statute the statuesque

MOIRA contending within smoke's billowing to atomize a stone-cloud call in the depths of new time hurtle curses acid rain upon the Forest while fucking in hollow mimicry over and over each a specter of the other's desire for universal influence they stoke each other's insoluble perversity to attain reproductive status the same as SEVLESMEHT stokes his carbon-burning signal in mimic of synaptic realities

my poet's mind is formed in awe of this pretense to power and will not let go its twisted upside-down sense til the nearest measure of my own by bituminous offal the purpose of dactyls and Daughters the length of spatial contiguities encased in the term of each cellular humming existence ZAS to hunt and destroy our inhalation certain and yet hidden seeming unattainable borealis our life-affirming thread our Law then usurped his gaseous hazy sense of ends and beginnings comes to the same within MOIRA

*where does this oxygen emanate* asks ZAS of MOIRA but it should have been asked by the other to the other but this knowing or seeming sense of knowing such question enters on the air and it really doesn't matter what role anyone plays anymore nor what answer to any question whatsoever

*excuse me pardon me* says SEVLESMEHT *but what is this we see in the smoke billowing our burning progress I mean what is this loss of production the caves by the Ocean's edges these beginnings endings driving comfort in vision toward delirious joy I have no calculation nor interpretation nor image for anyone anymore I keep looking looking I've even taken to waking in the middle of a sleep-inducing vision to find my eyes the bituminous sparks sent up the smoke-hole nothing new except it's not is it?*

*never mind* says ZAS so stately you'd think he was a God and not a simple projection of light upon the atomic theoretical now in throes of the greatest discovery ever within this species under the genus homo *never mind I'll have MOIRA win them over it's all timing never doubt it never doubt the timing ain't that right sweetie-pie?*

*oh yes timing is ...... so ...... temporal* and she sticks her finger between full lips sucking salaciously slowly her entire body curdles to white marble one with her throne the adamantine adytum of human history contained by ZAS-illusion gas shot thru with light and shadow in the showdown of the quotidian

AHNÁHR seals in joyous impaction another direction a kind of stone almost steel fortressing the cranial cavity of EKSTONISTIAN where birds gather in direction the cerebellum tic tic tic the Forest in praise of her they preen on the bough of a tree to her South the Plains of AHNÁHR the constellated might of his reach growing to her North arching underneath cold darkness of OURANIA the course of the universal to East and West her shoulders jut commencing tidal-like occurrences reproductive Law the mind more pregnant than the dark?

a balance a place where Nations FAERYS Men and Women come together in a kind of meltdown of time all of them acknowledged acquisition of what is communally hidden individually thru time

AHNÁHR wins with his universal con-stellations of New and Old worlds ZAS with his pretend world patrolling poll-utants isn't there a place for everything that lives accesses dynamism or is it all error and judgment thus contention?

Law or a Finger a Digit Psychic Vibration the bevel of gestating symmetry death life their course by the first call OKEANOS issued as possible age?

all the pitch for the brand was once a darned sock a simple stitch in time a ball of we-ave-ing in and out and back and forth and up and down folk art now a threat to the universal so sales-men dispatched by ZAS to the caves glare at the openings listening looking straining to understand what spun maybe crystalline affair something mineral then woof! blazing blason of Z attached to large and mighty catapultations out out out into firmament the horizon wow look those colors the sky lit by the act a continual bombardment the sales-men taking notes the most keenly aware adept on to ownership the ZAS-rod then falls to Earth marks a territory the edge of OKEANOS

the RED CIVILIZATIONS watch their men go into sales-training they see news the smoke-hole of SEVLESMEHT they see shadows cast by light made of things buildings churches corporations large small nations gardens species genetic multiples enumerations manipulation benignity weaponry stanchions slaves scribes computers real estate exploitation cash credit automobiles oxen ore deposits research development industry magic spells

ZAS pursues MOIRA to bind visionary broadcastings of SEVLESMEHT to the RED CIVILIZATIONS we have a hearing a shell or cave an ear which Oceanic swellings synthesize then command as if they were real waves a double helixing the entirety of living things for without ZAS and MOIRA AHNÁHR would not have gone to the isolate EKSTONISTIAN and pressed himself to her symbolic ordering

AHNÁHR has written materialized shown his one act with EKSTONISTIAN his instilling the dead skull by that sexual gore

EKSTONISTIAN AHNÁHR fucked as of the first the last the orders rejoice continually ZAS and MOIRA move into a bond with hatred eternal the ring upon her finger's slipped on and off a hundred times until her middle finger is raw what is she doing worrying pacing shouting at servants demanding they adjust the furniture only to have it be as unmoving as her vision then pleasured by the servants forgotten all their names some eunuchs *how dare this* EKSTONISTIAN *be circulated thru the world on a wind haven't I shown you what a wind is my gas-bag of a husband isn't that enough?!* *call the professional managerial hermeneuts to this place* *snap snap be quick about it*

*m'lady?*

*yes you exploradorations a retinue of this couch now we need a corporate trance huh that's good that's very good someone write this down someone get me a scribe I've just uttered another gem one of you exegeticals get a pen or pencil well here comes one of those Z-rods now* and she snatches from out a still cloud right at the rod's perigee a catapulted emblematic shaft thrusts it at the slaves *here write this down*

it seems like another planet SEVLESMEHT wants to take to the depths of a monkey-populated jungle at the base of this basalt-stoned region having relived his entrance to this world again sliding down rough stone in rain-storm crashing into vast underbrush as if a tree-top monkey casting wood vines other animals aside rending their bodies into bloody cadavers he is marching swinging his sight thru the densest jungles forests of the Earth on and on riving a path thru the wilderness where endless green the chitterings of little animals in protection soon he might come upon EKSTONISTIAN she's rumored to exist in the center the wilds he might just come upon her in fornication he's pulling undergrowth out by the roots now their dirty capillaries hanging from bulbs quickly discarded they form faces next the path he burns forward forms a larger face of ripped up thicket the creatures swift to have hid grab a tuber flick back the camouflage so a portent to the entire destructive rampage added to his shaman's skill

*SEVLESMEHT* here the ZAS-voice enters deep tone causes even those with a decent singing voice to choke it's hard to do dramatic voice justice but here goes *SEVLESMEHT go tell them of the brand from fires your smoke-hole the dawn of the horizon*

*EKSTONISTIAN's realm you must bring your followers to burthen this transition from a shaman's smoky runes into clear skies lay translation upon them show her as labor and they will have no need for knowing why they labor*

just a little bit further let me take aim then we'll have his whole oration in production *you've seen thru riving frustrated blind berserker soothe this vision televisoried toward total tumescent*

MOIRA has nowhere to go at last sees her window's form blast from outside moving into her brief visage AHNÁHR passing thru the estate thru voices cannot hear what they sound *daemon of the ancient world ZAS bind me to gold and silver mercury let me munch on the cream from your cloud-form master illusion*

*.............. let me feast time is ripe it's driving me insane the millennial a command beyond all from this shadow draw near enter become one with me rule me on this couch embed by me your clock .........*

the Daughters give out sighs their labors exciting the entirety of Earth

bubbly cool water the pool of her solitude her head gives out oxygen to the water Earth's copse-pool just before she surfaces her head her endless hiddenness a feeling never known or entered one of the many knowns she hears differently under surface reason so surfaces events an entire World the human World gasps shouting from her abilities the distraction of labor invested the human realm under-water hearing instinctively has no need to return the symbolic round and in that split second death the symbolic round needs become another round those emblematic caves ZAS-borne reality a crack at land's end the gaseous atmosphere pretending circumference the labor of these Daughters women molded by the surface expansion their natures eventually drift to the wild EKSTONISTIAN and the skull her gasping self

humans by their very evolutionary instinct blot thru philosophical contribution their charges inside mammon now we see ZAS rise to our shape and take our heart into Fields of Night under stars in a final judgment this is the time of ZAS and this is the meaning of our lives ZAS a magnet of eternal opposition to eternity itself now he stands at the center of the Fields conducting images dreams into his shadowy back and back of him nothing the contemplations of sight swallowed into darkness darker than blackest anthracite ore known deep within Earth's lithos we now become ZAS the numbering of the World vain calculation as if matter itself an age-old game borne by the tides of the mind tricked by reason the forces of wealth privilege ZAS owns any such dialectical in the night of a black insurrection

EKSTONISTIAN has come to surface of the copse-pool her eyes moistened some sort of preternatural pity a phanozoaelogical body from top to bottom begging the Daemonic thru distant narrow Forest out of nothing out of the air she breathes her titanic smallness hidden in the World's Forest begging the moist moss underfoot come bigger so vast her need reaching sweat now drools down her steely stony spine erected out of loam loess earthly composted humming center slowly spinning wobbling planet within galaxy at the edge of vast eternal space the chthonic urge tremors deep the calculating mind's dimensions

*Man's a dream I can cast away as my breath very quickly or in slow evolving emanations from surrounding immensity concrete relations the triangulation of chemical iteration the glint of refracted light mooring age as age within titanic memory titanic material investment an endless youthful speed an overpowering fuel to feed the world holds and releases my moment*

AHNÁHR thru EKSTONISTIAN from the shaken tree the Forest Yggdrasil of black bark-hide out of stories songs now singing letters hung from the vowelly trunk of her midriff

seedling cast in released captivity scattering into the pool or pond

the skull quivers and querulous ripples about its bowl of green life the duckweed frothing on its surface roots to limbs a newly formed head

sockets shooting green fluid carnal matter translucent reflective multiplication dark and light upon the center and midriff of EKSTONISTIAN the storied form draws forth a tongue or multiple tongues rising from submerged brain-stem seeking the symbolic within and without then sucking nascent oxygen up thru its buds cavities whistling netted bone the Earthly mycelial phanozoaelogical

ZAS when the one became two when destiny saw her face bugged out like slugs' glistening trails in the dark and into clustering explosive eyes dark and proud mouth alone a-quiver sibilant and charged with worlds out of exhortative inhabitated push and pull a skin he cannot join within his own so to overtake the temporal worlds he now goes toward madness the frontal lobe looking out over the asylum it rules the tympanum head a stone-age he alone unleashed thru gaseous innovation

EKSTONISTIAN brought ricocheting Constellations to this Forest to the time of the Gods the lived glory of AHNÁHR the mighty vastness of prehistoric space an abstraction of time in the ultimate sustained dis-unity

tillage of Earth in a vain dream of total interdependency in omni-distribution of poisons created from synthetic seed manufactured by gaseous illusions of power a substanceless regard for all Law or Language all things fruitless expositions of species now become extinct and raising the shadow of the hidden copse

OKEANOS maps from those same inlets to find her and cavernous splurges of his watery force thru neo- and paleo-temporal challenges to the sacrifice of symbolic wages all living things in the course of time calendricalized and counted by nothing hears the rumor of EKSTONISTIAN's imprinted tropism tendrils climbing into statutes and orders glyphs and diphthongs declensions locatives a futurity the Book of Time and Space as a batch of nitrous oxide will also be planted

the Poet leads by his black-body non-massed relation of AHNÁHR-EKSTONISTIAN-THERSEYN the World-Egg the other ZAS-MOIRA-? a forthcoming substitute for SEVLESMEHT two World-Eggs passed thru and thru with electrical wisps synaptic overlap

climatic helixicals of Earth the Forest phanozoaelogical communications thru AHNÁHR write and etymorph toward analogies hidden in matter a planet wobbling out of eternal coordinates the true expressions the temporal organization gravity our number even the number one zero defends the world in composition the New World ever arriving

AHNÁHR leans down from regions near the great mansions in the celestial north taking his emptiness into a martial array of darkness and sidereal calendricality and so this is the place where emblem and sign arouse the tortoise the snake both to write into the New World out of the Old a perpetual rutting or excitation of them

AHNÁHR at the entrance to EKSTONISTIAN thru the bolting electrical disturbance of a million storms the trunk the Tree which is memory hard soft contour the human symbolic source

*in I go to protest their unnatural love of mammon*

*a boreal wonder*

*rouses*

*Earth's pivot*

first sketch]

**ANONYXA***

notice the open deep vowel then sharp closes the mouth to the complete close the self performs of the throat in guttural spitting cavernous zone's incompleteness

tone catches vibrates the cranium guides the material consonant carries

*pronounced with hard **X** (thus)

.. ..

the self    formed hole    later the bag's tied    individual lost by being    the nature of being    allegory of that losing's    vibration    sound the wave    directions comes goes    cut-off    so    sew    sow    so-owe    the humming    sex's born to carry
    out out out out    the hole the

others    the hole    allegorical the hole    thing
    hard X    their chops    in time's    **thunk!**    self then thus merging to the zone or species "thinks"

••

in diaresis (the sketches go
    from this day to the next)

lust's change    divides unity vowel moves    sees *selves*    the cavernous echo-chamber

this seeming or actually extinct species
the fifteen feet deep jaw-bone and their curled-in legs

skull flung whole to the gaping    penetrant many   one 26,000 years before this moment    ancestral tadpole disconnecting in the current chords    cordage of currencies finished by being    an entire species by this too manied

.. ..    .. .. .. .. .. .. .. .. .. .. .. .. .. .. ..
.. .. .. .. .. .. .. .. .. .. .. .. .. .. .. .. .. .. .. .. .. ..
.. .. .. .. .. .. .. .. .. .. .. .. .. .. .. .. .. .. .. .. .. ..
.. .. .. .. .. .. .. .. .. .. .. .. .. .. .. .. .. .. .. .. .. ..
.. .. .. .. .. .. .. .. ..

latent in all language    there  language is THERE

womb    closed mouth source opens seed swims magnetic waves

sound or wave exposing her egg you see

skeletal showing
from the zone of our dig

bone

times the further down the dig the head the tool

egg's potency where and when sight won't grasp what it sees

consonance long-term memory the seed of matter

entrance to all symbolic relationship swims to join

26

and the matter thrusts **IN and … OUT** **IN and … OUT** **IN and … OUT** **IN and … OUT** **IN and … OUT**

gtkpq qpgtk p q t k g

second sketch]

## QAPTAKUSS

a desert in the eye sees now the turning seasons the rainy the heat the palm trees oasis the movement of vast sound carries sand in waves the chosen city of holes the fifth world's capitol Mesoamerica to enter the human histories right thru the center of the zone's historical as well as purely temporal shape the same the chosen world ordered by the infinite world of sound could have come from the ancient medi terranean or Earth's wind center of ANONYXA her being the mind then and there

he sees again her change thru time's duration
her zone the scale of all scales

.. .. ..

series of sketches each a part of one body the codes of the RNA/DNA the transcriptive world come to this newly historicized writing

each sketch's body diarestical movement marks

loses inheritance meanwhile **in**-heriting queer newness

third sketch]

### Creation of OÖND and OOM

ANONYXA's led to the hardened allegorical thru sexual desire of her diaresis body/ground now in pregnancy from an extinct time the new man the neander-like presents by *her* zone
as if all time
bearing within her a timelessness a shadow of the world to come?

some kind of fatalistic impasse where the twain will have to be missing as well as presented conundrum to the other the writer and reader of fate via each choice or command balled up by those bearings

PLNIPLOI one THERSEYN the other former the body become a dead extinct end and the latter spirit allegorical breaks from any other into timelessness diarestical challenges as afterbirth who is standing in whom? The synaesthesia of the zone become an eye-witness to itself thus telling time by the mouth of *her* species

call one stagnation/darkness but the other flowing light and conductivity potency of the egg bore surrender to the penetrant *thunk!*

*there!*

two different titles or times by time flow's *polemic* one of those magic sticks or wands erections ( I have *hearwith* done so

OÖND

echoing the latinate "wave"

*Unda* in dead latin then vowel rounding into O

*Onde* en Français    *Onda* en Español    and

opposite the stick or *wand* the cunt or cave

hollow womb

OOM

## fourth sketch]

### Extinct visualization

ANONYXA
chooses OÖND at first
discovers the use    discovers
allegorical dimension discovers the end
of time by his
stick or source in knowledge of the body of the world
enters imagination's zone thru OÖND    the endless intercourse
spent coupling produces many and varied views or multiple times as multiple
worlds    beings whose actions magnify    all and everything by the zone's limnality

I'll go in for further close-up:    populations    isolated universities    violent projectiles from the allegorical/physical
throws her being    a punch from/to extinct time shows her own extinction
thus our zoom too succumbs to the intercourse became the zone's inheritance

# fifth sketch]

## Mirroring extinction

title with an O and O will emphasize extension on the vowelie maneuver either internal or exiled positions of herself of her born twins in this world or even 0ut of it for how could anything exist without those two the whole thing which is

and for which these five have all the ontogeny any phylogeny might re-branch or whack off for fire by which to dig the entire circumference all the sweet and gone seen and unseen roots in a synaesthetic becoming the zone

even all    her name    carries

to O and    0

education come round again from tree to egg body to flow date to dated to pay the date or mark of time by her gestation

infinite finitudes    holes of the firsts to last    archived memories    symbolic autonomies    living formation

# ONÖNYXA

ANONYXA
Hears the chorus of OÖND and OOM
Depths of a worldly ignorance.

Was it death in her far-ranging stride
Seen thru eyes OÖND and OOM?
Was it birth of a wandering death
Instantly visaged thru motion small
Thin bodies foraging a way
Now ANONYXA tracks?

So in this also ears
Shape the known whose limbs
Vowel out her birth-stride.

Everywhere she rests she sees
Quartz the marble also limbed
Stone or everywhere's eyes
The Thrush with all the Jackal
Vulture predatory omnivore
sees our end.

Moaning hearing she's acquired
Incomplete depths the entire world
To traverse completely
Day or night thus finishes her trek

sad sustaining
Interpreter of the growing desert
Red sand a bodily shelf
Nothingness clouds her
heart's horizon
Outs out Being
under a silent air and sun she alone now hears.

Calendars arc a blinding need by the light
Beneath wavering eyes which darken time.
Beneath Earth the maw chants:

*What purpose what purpose*
*I forever broken and dumb?*
*I the dry desert a prophetic weather?*
*I the engine gathers my hand and feet?*
*I this joy mouthing*

*marking*

*dark extinction?*

Here is where measure
Extends to the infinite........
Here finite's mirrored self
OÖND stirs thru the underworld.

Face  clamped in motility
coupling naked OOM
soothing her foot's arch
the specificity of time's now fugitive soul
Defines by the dark
its signature

*The next moment's revealing:*

All gathering all
bring to her grains weeds
Heaping full the hole and holes.

Earth chokes its muddy furrows with many
Zygote Gamete
tether and assume their break-out
Her wet desert expands in their timing.

QAPTAKUSS chokes on the seasons by his mindings.
ANONYXA flies
With color of OÖND and OOM
Flushed out
over savannahs and mesas the table-top Earth
now an alien day and night-floor.

Composition to join the world's maw by holistic eternities!

And sight opens

admitting ANONYXA. Confessing ANONYXA.

*For the morning of night's passing past:*

Where are the paths?
They emerge from the allegorical QAPTAKUSS curses!
Gnashing loudly
Drowning this deserted engine with *his* domestics.

So she his death gathers there.

Thus  she thinks and sees by *this* event.

She's holding a pomegranate
Seed-studies now  mind
Taking universals within her lips
Moistening with vision
The depth of OÖND and OOM

marble mountain
Whose owl  scattering prey
Taloned thru flowing air  water  ice
Animals do indeed "know" themselves here....... .

*there* then furthering OÖND and OOM.

**Thus ONÖNYXA**
... surrenders to her own needs
Thus do waters  deserts  brushes and trees

thus QAPTAKUSS composes
Quarrels with shadows
Outlining features of an extinction

Thus     ONÖNYXA
    an impasse below QAPTAKUSS
Holding spirit in the sun he
                    cannot fully extol
            undone by his own lettering.
    But the water's animal motions
Tendering paths
     changing terrain she now wanders in and out of
Eternal rendering a singularity
OÖND above a dark flood (bathing limb's intent)
OOM   (inside the flood)
Mocking the weeping sweep
     of eyes and ears by primitive intent now
            sophisticated.

   ONÖNYXA rises
     toward that night vibrates the shaft of OÖND
And she's taken by the world
        of his mysterious anatomy
   as if it were a spear so sharpened
     murderous sigil not soon forgotten
       sounds out the gone wisdom of an entire species.

sixth sketch]    what I need to get here is the rise and fall of thought specific thought the one thing the zone comes thru a true acquisition where you are where I am *wherethere* weather    it was the fate of ONÖNYXA to realize the totality of her species and so the symbolic was born within her quite literally and this is where she went and why the passing from holistic nearness that mode of both sensing and mimicry made her move into the revelation into the gestation of the ages by the limbs moving to a storehouse of letterings or signings shapes or forms unknown in knowing held previously by one and one alone she now feels within her another

tracking relationships tracking by an umbilical thru all form and shape to all contained within the one which she beheld as mind    the timeless world thus defining an entire species thus leaving and the travel which ensues will always be the source of her species' futures pasts as well as its ignorant present tenses    consciousness measured by the unconscious in the same way the *un* is measured by the

imagination might have been pinned to the night sky as a constellation an allegorical dimension forever and ever

before any vision symbolized in the amniotic zone    we had eyes    millions of years in the different morphologies    but it was one uprising framed the orbital by its bio-logos a planet an orb in the stellar darkness    still by virtue of the species and what it holds as key to its needs as well as source-code to the zone of her gestational round    the stellar darkness doubly redounds

arcing significance of the sketches    a composition    not so much a one-sided string or series of notes    but what cannot be portrayed by tone or any one thing in a crevice of time shadow world which sends the stars' light into the mind of the zone's existence as it does the blackness of the deep sunless arc over the shell of the Earth

we understand language because of these two qualities    not always together they orbit around one another    in a sense

dark and light    quantities of them unseen also    we understand no one stage of their eventuality    existence is scattered in the broken mirror    the mind might be there shadow as light to put it all together    conscious attribute time discovers by lost flight the depth the endless universe

## SHIRU's PROPHECY BY THE LIGHT OF THE MOON

Leaving realms of spanning sleep
A World Image   reflected and inflected
Caught by the vowelly voice
    body's dreaming vigor
        newly formed SHIRU now intones:

*Head sound vain and vapor foretelling*
*Clouds weathers THERSEYN's forebears*
*PLNIPLOI will discover by decapitation*
  *ancient blood-rite and*
      *desert of ONÖNYXA's conquest.*

## seventh sketch]

### The table-top mind

mind-body connexion    they have to happen    my thumb hitting the space-bar
reached and there    to say    does that fit?    how to isolate composition itself to show each reach?
thus stories and narrations of our coming to light always stem from this splurge    spent surge    into protein silts and branches a coursing river of axonic nerve …

song's the new being    written on her zone?

## SHIRU CONTINUES TO SPLIT THE MOON

*Man will not be found in PLNIPLOI*
*But by the might of this natural world*
*Image its histories with science*
*Discover our spirit's diaphragm in*
*Unknowable manifestations of a will-to-power*

*Thus EKSTONISTIAN    toward fulsome FAERYLAND :*

*pulse now seen thru our soul in exhalation*

*Relative to the birth of ONÖNYXA*
*The desert floor where*
*PLNIPLOI*
*angers every shadow's form.*

# Processing the World-Tree

# Part 2

*the State of Mankind is the Future of Mankind so only thru and not by any Stage incomplete will you or I pass to become what for all time not just a little but all of it passes thru our State might become animal or temporal sentient cognition or fear of death*

# inalienable

## portion of the sky above and the ground beneath

makes one momentous Statement ride up into the affairs of all interpreted then by the mind or those in control or writ about with the impressed lintel's warning "abandon hope etc etc" which might be the place of Earth lodged in the mind as portal to horror yet use your own senses the State resides within itself as if it were an eternal crèche a crack evolved thru the edge of OKEANOS where the Daughters have had doubts then visitations deities which comprise our cloudy realm so because of this mystical triangulation a communication travels the World attracting interest just as a string of bait trawling the deep hooks and nets a hungry following

THERSEYN was born by the patient presence of EKSTONISTIAN and as those moments in the pool at the edge of a shaded world came to light so too the skull awoke from the rumor of the World's time

THERSEYN now steps over Earth reading thus in plain air the outcasts first then penetrating inner smoky camouflaged SEVLESMEHT RED CIVILIZATIONS redirected far from memory where man abandoned the State of Man for Stages of Man in reiteration of the material ZAS a gaseous aethereal realm based on the news tremors sent from OKEANOS and so THERSEYN stops walking and says *why does Man think why does he continue why has he not come to understand the might of AHNÁHR who rules the position of planets and is immeasurable your minds are broken wallets why doubt descent to read the future of failure why doubt ignorance why not get deep into it and iterate beyond any quadratic the large hollow the temporal immensities doesn't that make more sense?*

THERSEYN cowers in the coming rush of a fractal-based cloud but the blast cannot hide his skin from freezing pain he is howling into the intense inane clawing out deep-lanced rods unleashed by command of ZAS and into dimensions of no sense an inhuman pain begins to squeal and tear all reality with its signal of attack as if defensive bodies were actually in offensive articulation

ZAS orders his desert to grow and as the spools or rods the shafts and spears are spun and catapulted over the lip and arch of Earth the dry parched loam and loess turns to salt and sand and the pixelated is turned toward a vector-based plasticity and were this an electrical storm THERSEYN would appeal to the depth of the temporal and bring down the might of AHNÁHR to charge it with properly evolving dimension but this is a kind of psychotropic psychopompic blast of dry heat freezing all flesh an embranglement the earless universe intones

the hemisphere weeps within the State of psychopomp as if everything is leading to salvation redemption as if the ends truly the justification and history resembles all hindsight ever shot to gloom in fact time past becomes completely lost and this or any nation state's contained in a sheet or screen of night sails a fantastical realm just above FAERYLAND newly created to bring back the monarchic conceit land and sea and give the Soul to find origins in plasticity and re-ignite once again under the vast endless laughing cracks the empty building blocks the OURANIAN THERSEYN rouses EKSTONISTIAN to signal air thus quivering she sights into the sky the entrance to her involutedly extroverted being stretching the neck and to depths finding walls her still-extending limbs seeking *my head's exploded within and without but yet retains its figures in shade and light alike!*

EKSTONISTIAN's life the contour her body is the contour to reality consciousness between Fantastical and Earthly under OURANIAN sky-vaults and the Book will always continue in her desire which manifests human being from unbelief the center of a rotating planet where narrow and shunted identity never stalled and never started seeks its shadow in the wearing of dark light

meanwhile a stone face or wall come upon in dense Forest the sounds fell shadows ticking the immense underbrush or it was the animal-quick response which entered the scene looking back to the ancient stone a hole wherein nothing or drawn there drawn upon from air and the purling water-sprites the little stream over moss a mass of leaves a curtain from the other side water's expanding sound seems to lift move figures maybe shadows one with a very large rock or what in the form of unknapped stone he carries on his head as others watch and then falls under weight the gigantic stone while others bend and squeal and double in laughing attacks and too a hooting in the branches brings tree-monkeys carrying larger-than-life beans or nuts from the canopy howling with laughter hurling into the stage or greenery a stage being played by shapes and shadows an insect troupe portrays a kind of leaf or tendriled skirt and swaying hips to the hoots the hollers the whistles the shadowy crowd a curtain of underbrush lifts and the stone-carrying ant or drone enters and once again collapses to delight of the crowded stream-bank which quickly dispels into loud purling crash thru the Forest something falls to Earth but turning to the stone wall once again the hole which is now a face within and startles I took a step back the dead under my feet the detritus of this place cracks and the face flees into stone unrecognizable

THERSEYN hears the stars that hover above the Grove the deep Earthly Forest and swears within leap he pursues any further stepping over the planet must go over and into the OURANIAN for the unbounded world's receding empires and even thoughts *nothing remains but this word and the reading received and then issued thru the deepest EKSTONISTIAN's desire everything would also issue her so I ignite in sparks of crystalline veracious answering my own voice tells in the ear's holes were the first of me come alive to shades of the Grove the Groove of her EKSTONISTIAN's dwelling within so without seems to speak in OURANIAN vowels spasms of energetic combustion radioactive to the first the last borne by pure space and temporal immensities* … … …

MOIRA turns the prayer of the human moment shedding radiance within humming stone of her garment now humming as never before this new emptiness this new space opens in time begins to separate event from event her grip loosens she's hysterical in the classic sense so the measure of the human modulates at this dropping of the light in favor of an onanistic assemblage of marble fulsome stratigraphy the frozen molten adytum she'd once thought entire *the chorus the banting chorus the uptick the voices harboring fate we two ZAS must now render anew we weigh as if all of it all of us just this one place impossible impossible impossible*

ZAS stirs upon the summit of Man's World the symbolic he might catch and goes to ends of the Earth to find it as it was but part of him lost in devolution of his emanation cut down by regions beyond Earth and MOIRA and it is SEVLESMEHT now to seek and stir in visions from the tent in the growing desert the human populace so many more like animals his skin is entertained to maybe one day be permanent hide the material histories into some sort of sacrifice the symbolic in the form of a human straight thru the forgetful look has shed any kind of animal morphology so it begins with the trace of his hand-bone on the hide of the blue the trademarked beginning the end of his influence among the many RED CIVILIZATIONS giving a kind of primitive hope a kind of meso-innocence

MOIRA wakes in the chattering fold humanity dazed bewildered by ZAS's absence the engines of humanity sucking her teats of new worry intellection alive to time out of the very specter the Earth rising up her bounded wilderness of aether now nowhere to see any movement from ZAS this the horror then the tribute to the mind and this very trembling appropriation of all that once was known or spent on the marble couch in halls of marble races into disappearance the bigness and greatness of gaseous ZAS *we need to have words* she mutters and gnashes and curses *we need to have words we need to talk I'll make him see his error I'll make him back into the image he is we need to have words*

mankind now studs the Earth with slavish attention neither leaving nor staying but bound to attention brought thru MOIRA's lust in obvious admiration of ZAS his position an imposing and deserted now growing deserted vacated time

the animals come to light in the vacancy of his image

inane flickering smoke of fire ZAS-borne emanation the time of Man SEVLESMEHT carries with or without knowing any of it to the center of the RED CIVILIZATIONS a thousand cloudy realms organizes number energy prescient fear and the relief from fear becoming industrial ethic their unity echoes temporary disunity the calculating essence of speech a kind of total embodiment of truth its Being the multitude fires above the Human Maw and temporal shelf a kind of coral reef or calcined sea-wall so forthwith the entirety of vain nothing prepares itself thru the Mansion in the North by the sign of all symbolics in the dark deeps in the Celestial Mansions held thru 26,000 years of precessional rounds in codified signalings in fires by which humans bank their psychopompic conversations

EKSTONISTIAN gazes out becomes one with the sway of all these new emanations the State of Man flickering from recent specter of MOIRA the belly of its void burning increately some quick evolutionary movement mere stage-craft into permanence illusive time in captivity now from the spinal meridian compact expanding universal order as opposed to Earthly only she is a rising dimension surrounds MOIRA's minions even without being physically present each point of obdurate pain or pleasure in the constellated meridian radiates sound she cooed thru the Forest now here the light of a million screens blinding edges also human darkness where EKSTONISTIAN interprets the false actor by her meridian contraction expansion words which echo thru *eye-sockets only for our own interests nothing with anything other than brief blast we will find later our next interest string these to create the semblance of a State so over time we come to rule the State it will not be but a few eyes staged to look and those can easily be rubbed out in our grasp because we created what is seen and that is the best way to foment then gain control it is the best way to actualize we need the symbolic which has a chain-reaction influence among the living already in the works*

now the constellation SHŌÖNWU in serpentine light beneath AHNÁHR the spine of specter seething rumor the Stages of Man steals nothing void universal the entrance to SHŌÖNWU's Mansion sidereal coordinates of the martial north no longer a Nation the obvious observational or what with RED CIVILIZATIONS gathering in desert highlands attempting to grasp their record of fear and fading intuition it is the FAERYs gathering in dense green lowlands who once heard the Corybantes as they heard the entrance of the splurge of OKEANOS into holes the land in sight of Daemonic goals also smoke signals the plenitude of Gods and further Daemons thieving this whole compact of Humanity the endless mirror of universal error now within EKSTONISTIAN's travail where once progression of peoples yoked evolutionary fervor historical purpose now blind to the double eternal feature of thing and not-thing

MOIRA slides up to the Daughter's laboring and thrills to show a kind of victory by the rumor she seems to have performed *Images Categories Confusion and Time they're the mortal enemies of my own so purpose seduction into the eyes of Men usurping reproduction eternal vision they're mine and every time and time is mine girls it doesn't belong to you and you know it or knew it but just look at me and the endless transparency of these people must see it was me who brought them to you to show the new labor and what it might mean as a measure to be freed from any previous measure I mean after all it was my vast reflected home which came to light within the new mind just look at these adamantine poses!*

waves influx and tendril thru crevice and the holes the seams the latticework of the shore to tell the RED CIVILIZATIONS so resound in caves holes the wombs of this edge of the Earth the Daughters dwell and toil but it is also Earth's

OKEANOS a newly foreign final place what will it take to release this spell if even the spell's source has been forgotten and confused it can't seem to the ear to work yet this is just the kind of cooperative forgetfulness the RED CIVILIZATIONS must exact from the Daughters at OKEANOS

*........... pulsing cavities of the known world phenomenal sucking winds break up and seal down blow out and feel this tender bone of upthrusting vapor open your eyes in the blind time for the Earth has its habits now formed by combustible beats the forgettable growing semblance of these latent symbolic impregnancies at the edge of the world which works and works and all has become work driven into work a demand so all-consuming it invents an unreal place for the human animal .........*

THERSEYN revives and as if newly borne breathing the surrounding Earth also ready to leave ready to pass thru and looking over feeling for the place the proper time the sluice the interstice the slot or hole the work finding searching so the corners of the eyes of his head the World by extensions an invisible unity weeps frozen in place suddenly was it the epi-phenomenal ZAS whose wings beat like pistons of a by-gone era the gaseous aether the brain inciting all to chase the Daughters with every tissue of latent existence thus mirror also capture their forms in post-phenomenal wobbling de-centeredness of whatever and thus their future load of work thus their symbolic sacrifice to own from the beginning all time to the end each and every cellular capability so feel the walls to find news re-generation crowned from the walls as if a new species symbolic captivated ownership the capacity for latency it is an entire species this symbolic round motivating interests the natural world gone if not into this chase the mind-field the place the Daughters work within without any thought whatsoever as if to own itself to master itself it means to evolve regardless

let fly sighing shafts and so this has nothing to do with the relativity of rights the enumeration of rights nor right of rights or natural right these sighs directed to the bed of MOIRA even of one of them begins a terror all might have gained in the world is foisted onto women a pile of exhausted snakes the foot of her marble body turns the wild fur of a rabbit the moss on tortoise shell turns them into horror the mind over the southern hemisphere explodes now into a million red ice-cubes light's retention a solidarity and union a mastery and control both the same scattering thru the vectorized edge the screen of space now laboring Daughters erecting another rod's emblem the firing chamber the holes at OKEANOS catapult and thus the shore's outline into dirt inseminating gash upon the pedosphere

where the king or queen the bloodlines to justify an end to symbolic drift where the direction and insurrection war murder now growing by global conflagration frenzy to get the source the symbolic get at EKSTONISTIAN find her out all this as pretense to real war not just a game not just a poem all muffled unacknowledged ignorance this age but in evolutionary drift from center of a Forest now THERSEYN sketches under the hidden protection of time newer and older than any each little scratch in dirt on slate stone the base of hanging vines the World-Tree the Daemonic merging with sketchy surface the dark the scattering pigment made from tip of a choo-choo vine its crushed leafbud the song builds in general sound the Forest can't be gotten but by head above shoulders now humming singing on the melodic drift to occupy the one-time skull THERSEYN joins the tic tic the teet teet the screeching chang-chang birds marauded by vine monkeys sending warning into the Forest all of it seeming errant sketches at the base of the World-Tree joined with the music of THERSEYN's head let loose from any reasonable lineage or state's incline decline general Earth now given taken behind time in front of time behind histories in front of histories inside the FAERY's book might have been a drag or train of show hanging from hairy density a wooded area of fecund play thru serious mood within Mankind now become the legacy of EKSTONISTIAN may or may not have lived the melodic harmonizing all here from out a simple scratch a sketch so all insect revelations in FAERYLAND now in the spread wingspan of the chin-chin bug look he's drying membranous venous wings by small breath flowing into this hemisphere *El Niño* continual reminder this age no longer concerns itself with fishes swimming away from one another so *El Niño La Niña* blow in cycles from West to East lines paths of warm then cool breath thru trunks of wood the center of time and space

MOIRA thus naked and proud of the freaking change and now of dawn as if never one seen she then also flaring from the Southern Hemisphere striking her thighs in the Northern to run thru entire sham proceedings of the day and give it to the idiots all of them but good her body she's looking to turn to weapon but she needs ZAS impregnate her so her thighs glisten with ages of sweat then turns outward and it might even be a river of blood the sunlight upon blanched silvery white marble the artist's touch as such yet there she is pleading with ZAS at the edge of the human realm she wails from the momentary realization of sunlight how all is scattered and needs order briefly shows how much has fallen from her World and in that instant the realization of a child yes a child to bring the emptied temporal a being fulfilling her every past over and over and over and how much more she has to do to regain her non-existent glories releases the stellar goal of all Gods from her sight at once focuses length and breadth of ZAS escapes on a wind to the Northern Pivot to hide until into her fantasy an ecliptic of hatred in twinned weathering moments ZAS and MOIRA the World's religion its willful ignorance of the arbitrary nature of sign symbol the temporal folds within without the mortal universe strangled in a cluttered and force-fed mind of natural vacant deliberation selection drifting in that focus they both god-head and divine essence abhor now MOIRA's egg ZAS-seed combine no wonder they have quite suddenly ushered an intensely inane epoch ZAS settles her on a glacial lip within the backside of the Northern hemisphere panged exhalation by which news as code in the screen of the phenomenal a fog from so much panting breath and blood

above our heads the shafts of the emblematic sowers who thru many ages reading the *varves* the levels of oceanic splurge the unconscious systole diastole the nature of latent symbolic drift the one source a work-flow hurtles spindled knapped stone wooden signifiers toward the land and loam of ZAS gathers night and day in a purple and dim gold twilight by these explosive events OKEANOS works their hole and home eternally burning shafts thru streaking gaseous atmosphere toward face of this conflict contended time written in the Book of Time and Space this reproduction of a species bent on dominant valuation a rejection of recessive in-articulation and as if some kind of farmer's toil ZAS replicates himself in the form of Daughters they are none the wiser they evolve in the night air with the emblematic shafts rippling the purpled Z-fling toward solid Earth and when the rod's buried in soil shadow of a hound emerges or this is the beginning of a pattern of disbelief come to rule one day to overtake the Daughters will realize ZAS-borne illusions continue recede into temporal fold their true nature waits the gash in the loam or loess the sand humus at OKEANOS a new entirety thru Earth's vast enterprise when the crowning of the Earth's mantle begins in temporal light victorious universality consciousness ecstatic eternities the unconscious manifest species

ZAS surveys Earth's realm from his chest sends vengeance in the shape of time itself beginning again the play or projection of his own time as if his unused might to revive the coming fruition of MOIRA who in black and white rage filled him with her words and all kept the shimmering crystal of the sea awake within his domain yet never evolving to combine domains with any thus retardation in his phenomenal self a cinematic now reflecting deep into boiling Ocean's scintillance as the sun downs and ZAS pursues ever down-going strafing the waves' signals the terrible end of his realm or it is something flashing in the waters he tries muster a mirroring into the RED CIVILIZATIONS where they scatter in terrible temperature the desert a time-belt engulfs their providence rising in ripples heat-wave as mirage right in the middle of starvation

dream composes the center of the Forest tempting THERSEYN stay where now FAERYs settle elements in the atomic abode of Earth and his image goes out into the supernatural distances of eternity droplets of water eternal recognitions each exploding to the Forest floor in a pluvial epoch as the beat of time itself tuned from self-containment lost to the last realm the natural world Earth the planet now become an occluded kind of paradise must not spread thru rumor will for the chittering too much the chattering a kind of morality or law the fantastical language symbol the arbitrary capacity a fictional height aimed for as good the trees no longer canopy the rain pouring down to the very bog peat ten thousand years the almost schizophrenical apparatus of FAERY or wings rubbed together ceases flight within the world news reaches thru very matter all living things and death wings and image hearing every arbitrary capacity the ZAS-borne intellection cannot preserve THERSEYN in rumor for all time all rumor even tho he is traveling in the world and not by any one time-piece or image of time alone

ZAS now into shadow cool radiance lovely alive at prospect of his reflection in once-held creation stealing himself working himself alone he has learned *this isn't right but it doesn't matter it's too late and everything is or thought to be actually a two-part contention and I wish it would end but there's nothing anyone can do and I would let you know then like any to breathe forth THERSEYN will appear together with the emanation from my existent specter for MOIRA's gone to take my place at the horizon because she thinks it best and we are unseen by sight and that is why I'm telling you from existence as terrible or conceited as it might be I breathe forth now you breathe forth*

THERSEYN appears and the blesséd tree EKSTONISTIAN first swore her life upon in search of shade within the eternal within the boreal age comes this the age of Earth rumbling universal might not for majesty but for awe and wonder beyond the sensorium's reflection anew ...

and in this new wonder at beginnings and endings the foundation of her now blasts out flowery musk within the dew-moistened green planet she knows and we know she exists as she might have extended her own inexistence as if her existence a plot-point

and all the mated turn to wonder not with the eye or brain of that language but the furthering glow and sustenance deeply darkened secret folds of time and generation cellular measured epoch aeon biological time re-flects as composition guided by out-folding resonance from unknowns thru experiential meridian constellation stemming buds full upon a spine those unknowables joined to one body the source of all names

the body the folds of all chemical relations within matter itself the joy the unbounded joy discovers opening being opened thus the labor involved all rush toward the center of a web at the center the original hole the web now seen as the form working thru all things

not just belief but place exists this is the trickery of language it is brought above all else so place the place of our meeting together the rumor or moment of THERSEYN will continue this is time there might be life existence beyond this night air cools after heated lust the nature of one enters many this wonder to seek wonder no more discern existences the meridian expansion of space even of dark interstitial space the interpluvial time

*... ... stand back you mere images of man's void ... ... I am coming in that instant when the grand umbel of AHNÁHR over me then over everything will accomplish will seem to be within the small so the main horizon of time which no one owns in that moment the temporal weight the universe will exhale an oxygen so rich diamond-like*

*minerals within its viscous beat will sap the birds and the bees in fact it will be the re-creation of the birds and the bees … …*

now ZAS sparks storming whirling emanations eidolons space time cozzens develops works workers Daughters fingertips rally scrounge Earth's surface continual denial traveling shadow speak Book Man future present distant THERSEYN hearts knowledge darkened wear pretenses offences primitive world vision motion action mind invisibility contends ownership sanity lust MOIRA womb semblance seed taught history sowers emblematic lancings lip coiling wormlike reflection temporal unfolding embolden satisfied incubate eternity something feeling hearing calling sighing dying

*might it be that a within without a without could and might the absolute carry the future to annihilate all other futures thru its visage isn't this an ability above all other abilities the place of the reproductive as final productivity a superstructure known or yet to come?* thus MOIRA understands the loam loess the edge of the Northern Boreal while afterbirth enters the place put whereby to enter the new age and counting

THERSEYN stands within containment of clouds to determine the depth of vapor howling dissolving the cloudy canopy tho as any impending storm still the inevitability of approach a warning once again he has no way to finally make it in the world either of gods or of the productive capacities now roiling with an errant rumor sans any sense human habitational holistic communicative his head bobs again sending out a signal to the symbolic depths his individual morphology the contour of time itself

EKSTONISTIAN pitches sways disappears immensity vision time canopy green temporal manifestations bombard seasonally woody rhetoric capture dirt arisen armor limbs combatants gloom Field Night clutter peace junk epoch shrapnel energetic progress springeth unknowing

*might it be I carry the reproductive as a final productive capacity of all human capacity and have been both seen and then rumored thus?* THERSEYN in the mental battle with himself a character of science versus the Book of Time and Space

thrown down to the feet of MOIRA whose marble flesh now green a kind of fecund moss a lichen from the bogs of the Northern Boreal rises the visual realm as new superstructure this hemisphere THERSEYN thus his bobbing little head MOIRA quickens quite suddenly to a scream and blows thru the prophetic chamber of his ear right out into the vast constellated night his future in the OURANIAN sparks lightning quivering capacity the half-life of all matter so the power now upon him from it and into his need grows under MOIRA's monstrosity a doubled opposition vast hearing in the one a position of infinitesimally small seeing in the other so that looking down thru all ages only one note seems emerge playing or striking itself over and over in that realization MOIRA confounded by an existence should simply not turns to coo and murmur her newborn the entire future all existence human animal mineral even the inorganic which she assumes intimately

THERSEYN staggers in a realm of disbelief their influence MOIRA toward ZAS with newborn PLNIPLOI this three-fold spirit their child rearing once again a bygone world to end this world in its beginning

THERSEYN toward EKSTONISTIAN who would have a dwelling under the shade of AHNÁHR another three-fold apparition of the world ready to contend every age might come at them surrounded by blinding light blind darkness entwined by cool shade within organic issues up and out thru the seasons the disintegrating calendars they once were charged in this moment to defend it from without

ZAS swears at this gaseous effluence within the organic as something he cannot control so he questions once again his nature his realm so to speak and rages at the image of THERSEYN coming up out of time rages toward the storm he created and whirls above trees cracking essence thundrous blinding arrays of atmospheric reflective cloudy screen in order to blind and thus enter into confidence THERSEYN

momentarily within the Stages of historical time a ZAS-borne emanation eventually THERSEYN himself the realization of non-realization overcome with illusion of one simple image suddenly he is in a desert to writhe within stranded unable to assert his own this retention begins build then quickly on a whim a sirocco over the sea sands now red the black sands join rain falling within caves holes at OKEANOS pollution which is heavenly the Daughters wake incorporate further within their catapultations

EKSTONISTIAN in blissful sleep or almost inexistence an epoch either here or there becomes the realization of further control the primitive lusts desires which contain the symbolic revelations and the plots of time a meridian heretofore unrealized

THERSEYN upon a desert plain the spectacle of atmospheric séance magics as if in disappearing from the power-play somehow surrenders to the age the erroneous assumption of State one storm this kind of evolutionary dynamic an anger vendetta itself comprised of inexistence camouflage a pretension of itself without another

now the Daughters receive AHNÁHR a breath from the oceanic intense subaltern issue *this is but the Daemon's visage furthering natural articulation begun interstitial musings vain hollows forever yearning by the chance-held rod you come upon every so often will be prolapsing to the great OURANIAN arch and from the order of matter in a half-life determination the electrical relay we disperse is only the meridian constellated contours time itself simply because it sleeps within all it knows forever and … … …*

MOIRA turns to her followers who are held within her emanating horizontal a multitude pronatal and retired *swarming bodies of angels vanquish the rumor of AHNÁHR each of you from this blazing horizontal now multiplied by the marble couch the tableau I strike upon an inner ballast the World from highest to lowest a geologic salt-peter which will now burn and erase any in a white blinding instant by its golden instant its alchemical appeal*

the Daughters now of AHNÁHR speed work in time to OKEANOS rimming our world with delight calls forth ZAS a two-fold semblance of the natural world hidden even from themselves

THERSEYN sends signal from his cranium to the bounded tribes the tributaries the braided post-glacial seasons of lands enlarging his foot-step over the planet the Stage of the reproductive enduring the productive capacities evolving humming to undo Earth's frozen ages with the mineral electric forms hidden and camouflaged by the deep precession of human fallen time

recalling or turning over in the cranium this walk this step these strides the cool darkened radiance leaf-dense monad Forest Boreality the symbolic unconscious round any productive center thus summoning times radioactive relays universal moment turns the key in the bones

## eighth sketch]

from the arabic *shi'r* breath-force surrender to the dark night the place of a standing reception the proclamation oracle delivers

poetry (derived) the word

*shu'ur* (arrives the vista)

Orphic

## ninth sketch]

**SHIRU**

here's our author now the unexpected
        San Juan del Crux        whose
soul and the bridegroom because there is a call from the male of this species toward the soul's lost aching inarticulation

**AHNÁHR & SHIRU**

SHIRU's male    thetic agglomeration the glottal hears heard hearing
        meets the soul    she-mind    the apparition    specter of stage and state

specter of stages and of its state    AHNÁHR
    incoming as if a finger to the soul's text
wide-ranging wandering    returning tides    moon-substance
    water meeting hardening land    dry seed-stones stock taken and taking and took    the points of time starry groupings cross to the sun-vacated view thus sounds

"water turns to milk"

## The new canticle

*after San Juan de los CruXes*

in homage to the influx of combinatory numbers
figures and mathesis to obtain the Moorish influence of design
intention in a world of alienation and cosmic dis-calculation or cant

SHIRU
over wave's architecture
so the song's a circle
Or it is as in the zero a non-sum
Purpose of our religion
Thus civilizations are divided
And as the moon divides the sky
a series of months as sketches
Divides within itself a sickle accepting
Influx of starry penetrations     dark pregnancies

Between PLNIPLOI
and Daemonic jealousy the Intellect
Raps the feet of all men
To trip them up
bump their falling heads
Length and breadth of creation re-joining.

How many heads must fall
Before PLNIPLOI decapitates himself?
In each night and day the birth
Or pregnant potential awaits his special end
Species extinct but knowledgeable
Dispossessed of dream     a science of self
Comes without ONÖNYXA.

That they cannot see
    *from* clouds
        the coming *form.*

From the soul of AHNÁHR
    voice's strange protest
Spells upon animal-cunning speed
Delivers a presence to its world
Giant might singing to *his* temporal lover ……..

                scales
which weigh us
all gathered

Is it God
Or Daemon
*Nephilim*
Cloudy awe
Speechless
igniting?

What interpretation of the world
Enters this house
Crossing bowelie passion
Beyond windows and doors in
cellular disguise?

Animating     seeming to want animation

A sure sign
Earth has formed
*Salnitre*'s living mined solitary illusion
Opens peripheries in time
A motility of Being
seen and then read
by another like me.

SHIRU calls to the eyes of AHNÁHR
And toward rounds of love his song sings:
*Shot with your strength I wander*
*Singing    I overtake your temple*
*And thus speak within her gone sense*
*The rumored sense of EKSTONISTIAN ONÖNYXA's cousin*
*Whose future will entrance human time*
*Now*
*see her distant arrival never-ending. . . . .*

*This cool new fury finalized the heart!*
*You    AHNÁHR    bring the zero sum of days*
*Counted    captivated    humming into matter!*

As a galactic formation lost
Shows to the waiting voice its echoic dimension
Learning vast tablature
insurrected from the ear's need to know

itself (as it was unsung and hung in the dark where some occlude by such "castration")

:

*The eye I AHNÁHR know*
*And yet do not*
*Reflects*
*A lost universal.*

*I know the loss.*
*I've desired temporal power*
*Somehow seduced*
*And rise by your holding hand*
*within new depth*

*And fall     far away     voice*

*threatens me with echoic play*
*whereby the silence*
*once held all*

**The Author:**
*Is this the feminine illusion?*
*Is this the other?*

*Am I the material essence of love?*
*Am I un-ending resolution*
*The song of five sparrows*
    *beside one watery body panting breath?*

*SHIRU   come on!*
*Speak once again*
*You've got my attention!*

**The Reader:**
The forms of the world were taken by SHIRU
Wed to love's desire
    hermes–like   hermaphroditic

A million mountains of seed beyond us

So that word of AHNÁHR be given away

Given to all anatomies. This composition anew.

Material necessity     "natural" desire

The center     never far from capacity

eternity

to lie by love's stalled withholding.........

## tenth sketch]

these two males       now gone to own time as their own
could as well spring from fe-maling entities (rocks say it also stones eggs carried in land's anatomy)
but this was SHIRU's great break-thru

so

these songs of the soul to the bridegroom go back and forth between two densities born from *his* thought       there's a finding of the mind in particular to actually naming it       there *is* a synaptic bridge
a neuro tic   &   a seminal tic

# EKSTONISTIAN

Desert stretch of an enantiodromic search
Savannah'd
          savannah'd ONÖNYXA
                    toward further evolution

Kissed by the sun
Fed forested mirage
  horizon of sight's symbolic sweat

Her image
  among those she's left

      a twig in the cornea

Her language now outward bound      mobile    modular

    holistic once again I stand

          stoned      pregnant with lost eKstasy

                    losing it out of doors

        eKsapted      eKstensive      eKstolling

## eleventh sketch]

pressing concern
composition pressing organic essence hence the other things become the center of the poem when they become the center of themselves but this pressing from one composition and yet we are the sum total of more than one extinction has grabbed the essence of one hasn't it and that's the whole point no? in to relentless focusing a gone-to-the-end-of-one-deal

each thing's a planet or sun or star again both AHNÁHR and SHIRU bear the world *and* from me *and* from composition without the reasonable attainment of a compositional truth because these things interchange their own natures not the pressing concern of an overall oneness as some sort of great zen-like american adaptation of what it did not grow in acculturated compositionings in other words you are I am cent ers centerings
defininings of ex-is and ex-Os

twelfth sketch] is it the singing and the speech of humans destined to hide in the singing and speech of the physical animal who sketches a territory and enlarges and presses the necessity for work?   not the trail of a reality or intimation of another reality but a working born from the animal nature of the human   it's simply not possible to have any further realities without an insanity driving every inhabitant out of their hole in search of their animal other

hence   these sketches are about new names
traced by the "other" (of us) not any other   but *the* other

time moves on and I become familiar with thought and so to renew commitments to feel them and taste them and know everything here   and so in this way to know everything about states or names these anatomical sketches follow a hiddenness of their names or ages   but of course it's amplified or it should be amplified by the branching limb in a stage of growing or the web in a rough circular away from the center to hold it there

I must follow the dream behind all human things uncover the falsely or strictly human hole

people really inhabit and what part of their souls are completely unused   this to be got out by the embarrassing use of a "square" diction and syntax a vowel in love with its own *boing-round*   extending into a capability or a memory or intimation of what could occupy this place thru its empire in love with all power

I carry phrases   they expand from our other   and yet those phrases do not exist for mere vibration for they go down into the world like ANONYXA did to become ONÖNYXA and was that just nonsense and if so what *is* non sensing?   sex   the union of the physical and the desire for the continued physical a way of fulfilling the physical?   but it has a scale which is told thru the gestational

## thirteenth sketch]

history shows us the domination of the human intellect both morally socially and in extension thru predication a dynamic as well as machination an extension of work so that any indominate or recessive trait is not brought to light but by a kind of twisted or mis-used analogy

to be an expanded subjectivity
worldhood whose new frequency issues forth from defense of that world     yet there is a scale or weight within the species
a wavelength science cannot touch because it incubates its signal within the reproductive capacity of Universal Being (thus time theorizes onto itself in jealousy's chamber or cave)

## THE SONS OF OÖND AND OOM

What you call cognition
Churns in the fields of a galactic magnetic
Defense of an after-glow beautiful
Livens prophetic coruscation
        out of Earth's precessional axis-tree.

Beats against a mortared a dead world
Unresolved    they go    to meet their parent
Anaesthesial remnants of millennial sacrifice
Fragmented horror    knowledge    retrieved
Thru conscious and willing surrender.

Sons of OÖND and OOM
Seize the path
ONÖNYXA took.
                Fire thus
        rages from their inherited extinction
Industrial ethic    encompassing axonic
And in four mirrors
        multiplies tongue-body manipulations:

  the Sons    split in pursuit    of the dark
Pursuit of the bright oncoming attire of endosymbiosis.

These two repertoires    these two models
                of extinction.... . .

Power to the phenomenal world      prolific
   and the Sons of Light contend
Amongst darkly human anonyms

From the forward moving forehead
The forearm's stated goal

Staged in evolving branches of the World-Tree's
Bowelie depth    the unmoved root in
            prehistoric ooze.

fourteenth sketch]

we've been born to witness fraternity and contention from resistance to SHIRU
the daemonic storm ensues in neurotic contention to all these within the state of
man's very Being mythos portrays unravels time into a staging area then back
to its state all within the veins and capillaries of an amniotic scale this might be all
EKSTONISTIAN's doing the apparitions of these movements sketching a territory
that is neither now nor then but is there and extinct according to the temporally
incognitive non-retrieving retrievers

two egg-shaped containments overlap each with its three inhabitants and as
bodies formed or unformed made or un-made move up to the walls the epidermis
the shell of the two oblong circles they become one another in the overlapping space
of each a long narrow almost spear-like trunk the center-space of our canvas

## Momentary

One    tolling in universal monologue
The other    multiplied from the towering World-Tree

AHNÁHR
    where EKSTONISTIAN'S presence portends to safety
        duration of his universality
     shadows her outgoing and longing
        to be her true length

            finally

  toward the copse or inner shady glade
        of the eye's sidewise slit

        So    natural her imminent escape-act    a time-splash
        Above man    within overlap or kiss of AHNÁHR
        A shade himself above men    first to echo love
        Turned the world down and    in one moment up-surged
        Columns of mist    the aether dreamt
                    smoke and fire

        Cloudy    horizontal reason cannot dissuade.

# Processing the World-Tree

# Part 3

*song and saga and the muse necessarily end with the printer's multiplied goal the screen's enumerating synaesthesia gone now thru-out the entire world instantaneously the necessary conditions of epic poetry vanish within this global splurge thru industrial dynamics which even here show merging individuals in a shared re-generative natural seeming into and out of the Paleo?*

*thus time's a visage a post-time while at the same time activates role-plays emergence a proto-historical mathesis each individual bears impinges imprints upon others the new song and saga*

# RED CIVILIZATIONS

## now seize their own knowledge

the two-fold semblance of light and dark folding historical movement ever to replay Earth's FAERY paean emptiness nothingness a mere drop of dew

tribal slight differences ethnicity morphology still the genus Homo they into many this process for review all must agree the relative newness slowing for approval while semblance of MOIRA they ratify by marbled stance within previous age

EKSTONISTIAN involutes to an icy sphere raising in thirst an empty cup from frozen dark mud the Forest floor crying in terror all the twistings turnings the age all of it worthless senseless somehow within unknowing durance artificially maintained inorganic distributions her face tears streaming flowing sweat her body naked collar bone receptive to the measure drops now beginning to be uncovered she'll perish be tossed aside cursed before killed the world's inattention now coming to a concentrated effort and yet THERSEYN exists

surely she'll perish without protection of AHNÁHR she falls to the ground giving way as dreams also end for the might of AHNÁHR over Earth foremost the interplanetary OURANIAN evolutions control fate EKSTONISTIAN now to grow out of this coolest darkest place the planet she must understand energies the fold of Man's civilizations a billion she will let travel and the global search symbolic war mined silver stolen gold shipped thru oceanic storms landing business transactions Charles the Fifth the many war's payroll debt consuming the Old World for New the first moment distance discovered

THERSEYN leaps for this void so seeding an a-voidable moment *beyond the State of Man thru cranial signalings thru memory I go to find this missing place the world by fate of one species a song or staff notes falling forward not back .........*

Contingencies Categories Characterizations! Powers Thrones Dominations! the weight of AHNÁHR works within throes of OKEANOS by the bounded world by states of an incompetent species his unbounded sense signaling martial position a mansion and every symbolic agency within the OURANIAN the ultima most the pivot of AHNÁHR churns in the deep!

not only social hierarchies within and without mineral and electric charges time and space the chemical codes memorial decisions the protozoic positions transpositionings over arch of Earth by Daughters the eternal womb OKEANOS roaring for power Ocean the end of conflict now ZAS flies toward in fulsome recovery of MOIRA *marbled flesh marbled flesh powering intellect hurry the waking lids the glittering glimmering sea blinding flashes edges the waves all of it within us the supernatural out of rumor superstitious clouds spread the message your coming boy-god-man who'll finally answer all this blathering conflagration these contended images without proper injection thru temporal Earth an eternal void a mind to end all other look look the screen of the ocean flashes from pole to pole now faster than ever before!*

EKSTONISTIAN in mind rumbles over and beyond the fantastic Oceanic the pool the Forest lost to THERSEYN's whim as it grows thru the cranial within and without holes and into and out of time a power or mode of ignition excitation for her the oceanic thus news of the world the fate of mankind nearing

Daughters feel the rumor spread thru-out work-stations living holes echoes a Plain of land endurance brings forth vegetable memories connexion from broken soil the World-Tree symbolic language the search hunt hounds tearing at meat all of it now on a stream from the depths of matter the navel of temporality

the nearly extinct homo sapientia

OKEANOS had run thru in a splurge of foam watery force the RED CIVILIZATIONS remains in desert the dried out regions one found now all hear or see report legs bent at the knee up into the neck skeleton a few scraps of clothing broken vessels indented dust dirt was he sleeping were his arms up under his head a kind of pillow dreaming far into his own death?

highland dry cave a tall hat bead-wearing tribal leader baubles symbols of authority now only groups of bones draped in sack-cloth flesh decayed blown away dust his stature from upright ambulating time synaptic possibilities captured by barren echoing Plains the table-top scape the upper reach Earth he'll never know

remnants of a feast cannibalized remains hollow in the once frozen ground nearer ocean's lips the few bones a group traveling toward dry desert heat out of time turning to waste each other's meat thru teeth hungry maw the image superstructure the blindness an end to work permanent end the dribbling blood sucked mouth and tongue spirit sacrificed gnawed marrow licked free annihilated soul one full gut choiceless decisionless supernatural lust

yet other skeletal piles an abandoned ravine dumped fallen subsident red country foothills bones a mass die-out now signed extinction the salinated calcined stone Oceanic promontory peaks memorialize contoured edges Earth time a fallen herd of aurochs approaches

Daughters of AHNÁHR move the planet thru purple nightlight greeting OKEANOS sigh and erase the new dawn their work to travel from fingertip to breast to arm lung and fling! go the rods of ZAS yet with tasseled remnants tri-lettered spell waving in the wind blowing atmosphere weathers of a wild energetic rapport fossil and form substance and insubstantial number by degrees delight in the thought of AHNÁHR beyond industry by virtue of THERSEYN's bobbing head in signal to the Forest at the center of all ages contentions

heart muscles quivered in desolation cranial captivity these women move now time against time now new time dirt and shadowy green underground marine subaltern rivers World's resolutely rebellious nature pursues insurrection thru each and every age each and every place each and every time

SEVLESMEHT digs into the dirt to bank a small fire watching pictures of ZAS-borne intellection taking disguise after disguise to compounded limits forcing prescience smoke rising thru his tent in rings each billowing smoke a blackened silver redaction the Earth become historical mission an onanistic version of lived time

signals moving thru the skull of THERSEYN ricochet back thru the OURANIAN to Earth travel the religious visionary teaching renewed thrown out the world incubates in midst absolute doubt to find its center all holes taking his cranium round no one predicts portray except within his own at the very center

EKSTONISTIAN's lengthy embrace eternal placement as both shade and gone body the State of Man Plains of AHNÁHR one picture of two at distant ends connecting wavelength each realization universal within the work of Daughters reflecting from sound diamond flashes Ocean they inhabit whose contours are time entering all work catapulting drive industry intelligence reproductive human tissue to incubate production a kind of quotient in the seasonal round a pretend ownership generation to generation now thru causeway of an abstraction the narrow channels of need blind desire great tragedy disappearance an image depopulated not so much this work which keeps apart animal natures the symbolic keeps to the Paleo anything might fall early or first form every being might become unconscious prone position the very first the position the direction pitch constitutes even tho rising relative pitch these changes fall and as they do the World-Image the Paleo potency a kind of paradise a glimpse glimmer a glance in the void

gorgeous attention within a long-winded composition essential structures symbolic relationships attendant cycles times must add the tragic fact nothing no one but a coin to blot it generation after generation

upper reaches the Plains above OKEANOS echo all relation all composition the Book of Time and Space all can be erased pitched toward Earth

ZAS enters the marble adamantine pose the judgment of MOIRA so Daughters sing while they work released voices without doubt hesitation an unconscious rendition the World's time

THERSEYN symbolic attachment to each brings the superstructure central problem AHNÁHR addresses thru drift of contention addresses from martial position in SHŌÖNWU mansion filled with sublimated excitations

......... *from* time is *to* time toppled *thru atmosphere of Earth in planetary exchange in foundries of matter imagined by Man's industrial dream never attained but by me* says AHNÁHR now thru the skull-image of THERSEYN

SEVLESMEHT begins his mating trill rubs his body with the balm of bushes to rouse the interest of some female of his species his visions the root of his own pushed into pure animal see him as an ape now lathering for a date

EKSTONISTIAN thinking to herself she begins to climb past the lip the edge of OKEANOS *will never found anything mightier but a leap thru totality finality the image man needs to see .........*

AHNÁHR rose up within EKSTONISTIAN a fate greater than human time above helixed time biosphere a destined reception his dreams without which nothing the human realm forms attention of form so shadows of the World were MOIRA in adoration of ZAS then vice versa stolid light marble substance the rumor of matter stolen by screen of gas in this aeon the FAERYs cling and hold the human brain aloft chemical necessities communicating now ever clearer within time

layered effulgence ZAS and MOIRA the two-fold compliance toward rebellion the very reason for war the matter itself within and without the human fold winning absolutes of appearance and disappearance before temporal might of AHNÁHR has hatched the trembling begins at the lip the known World all now in thrall to work performed as if this séance of things and human time were at an end

EKSTONISTIAN extends to pluck a leaf one last time the FAERYs rejoice her movement the embodiment of knowledge within the Forest all now all is taken

each star

drifts in expansive dark

Earth delighting the mind by the digits of Daughters their number circumferencing a World-embalming spirit breathes inclusion conclusion all things opposites fragments from THERSEYN's recognition toward seasons toward temporal mappings the Earth's shadow radioactive within work's spectral self-awareness falls blinded by feedback OKEANOS the material pump shimmers molecular element unknown to the world's orbiting inhabitants

## fifteenth sketch]

evolves within gestation of ONÖNYXA / EKSTONISTIAN    the very population of the Earth within the human mind and limb of those two

one day the penetration of the Fifth World will bring forth a mirror-image of what they are and the battle or contention of one anatomy will wrestle with the other over the vast growing unknown no matter their similarities within the imprints of reason    so the eye needs see itself to engender itself

within reproductive capacities    fate is wed one primordial to another and is thus the meso-near a logos grown and twisted thru ages out of medi-terranea    now signs point to the primordial neo-reflective capacity of

**PLNIPLOI**

thru daemonic agencies of a reproductive freedom there stands the figure of PLNIPLOI whose very nature flattens the multi-dimensional canvas suggesting no access to any zone    his is a feint toward the calculative in guise of a theo-logical lust for power and empire    i.e. the calculative

based in his own will the all knowing    so the time is coming for his complete reign the newer version of the unknown    the primitive

# sixteenth sketch]

human philosophical proposition has been restated within the emerging work

our life is more than the proposal's words not so simply the Other either but it has a seedy characterization lost to the annals of seed culture and the area for the working sketches out from the newness of the work all contentions as well as axonic access

ZAS flies into the construction imprisoned there and all substance of the world of man and nature communicates Daemonics of the human spirit which was simply once an apparition of a thing in an academic setting rumored to be a life philosophy in the movies and on television such bunk it's amazing people haven't committed themselves wholesale to membership in SAG

seeming the sources of feeling mere matter is of the realm of the sons of OÖND and OOM marking an insurrection from the individual in a community of work's signature pivoting and penetrating wobble a script written by the hand of our species the precessional activity of the Earth over a 26,000 year cycle each and every day returns this new calendrical evolving

## ZAS ÜBER ALLES

SHIRU my hungering titan the navel of mankind
Come from progressive might
Now he too interdicts the universal
Eating his heart forsaking seeming vacated apparitions
Studied as the balance of monies
Studiously studied (to own the book thru "balance")

Now taught to gut membranes of the noumenal
And bind once green juice into sfumato fire
Singular remnant of the rumor of the mind drawing forth

Thus
sketching his own pneumatic prophecy by neo-doctorate:

*Sons of our Liberation and the movement*
*The Fifth World's polis and the growing*
*Caravans of inactivity by evolution's pivoting symbolic*
*Quell your spirit*
*in the matter hammered to submission!*
*Remember toads tortured the insects de-winged*
*Boys of small pomp's transmogrified circumstance*

*So within your number*
*On an insubstantial battleground*
*All chemistry and bubbling elixir of physics in the mind*
φύσις *before OÖND and OOM as to our first* πνεύμα

*I am become ZAS*

*risen from the land*

*Atmospheric*

seventeenth sketch] from self all that has been given to the center-space now in contention as the work which takes up every question and answer is thus the place which is NOT the assumed place the world itself now become one in the place of these cognitive dissonances then to sonances an art for the ages or scale of gestation from Meso-near back to the Medi- and then the Paleo-far

in mirror the world has become a hermeneutics of self and the re-turning forces of allegiance to physical love even in dotage and yet to be teased out of that by the very same dotage

stare into the ignorance of this reflection and symbolic ovoid every ratiocination in contention now born from the ignorance the ignoring of measurement from one world to another

**New daemonos a temporal ovoid formation**

the anatomy of this allegiance travels and is a zooming thru time and the modularity of all knowledge was secured by ONÖNYXA led by the *ont* the movement of our species time all of these forms born most probably in the ovoid mirror within the gestational

anatomies in want of circulating blood I acknowledged

Daemonic free-borne melding temporal dance EKSTONISTIAN led further flesh became shadow a further proof of the heart human frames in thrall to the heart's two chambers within Daemonic forest whose dimensions grow or shrink according to investiture of the work's rounding toward no work and stasis

a cataracting green moment or means within the ovoid mirror moves slowly in the morning to undress herself for the entire species in evolutionary movement a small copse actually a small thicket of dense bush we have yet to ascertain but it is of a flower's lifetime and I am in the center of its up-folding color

thus the patterns of free-borne intelligence are like a snail-slug looking for its lost shell-nacre its iridescence inside to reside in the smooth crease

knowing in a brief glimpse the larger projectile motif of biological capacity formed in the Paleo

## eighteenth sketch]

the nation relies on fossil fuel        a ZAS-borne age

as if history were turned backward into itself as an ignoring of ignorance        its mammon roars for *alchemical* contention        as if it were love and eternity and paradise and hell        it seeks the sources to found something of value out of        to activate them by the lighting of the fuel        all order now to save the orders which are dead or dying seeks this re-sourcing

## Ignition

PLNIPLOI'S city
Exacting tribute from the sons of OÖND and OOM
From the daughters of ONÖNYXA.
    Are you inspired?
Would you risk high-flown speech
To reach the shallow depth intelligence now seeks?
Have you the contemporary cadaver
And so for a mouth the true character
Want's contemporaneity needs?

            Each head falls to belly of the sewer
The Fifth World's meal-time
Universal in its conceit to frame
All by the will of PLNIPLOI's
Ensigning λόγος. I reach sans reach
Into the form to mouth
Every thing the same.
    Yet ONÖNYXA flies
In song thus waking SHIRU by deserted
Words the song
Enters wave's epic
Turning tides in cavernous shells of speech
Continuing from the spell of PLNIPLOI's ploy.

For this is the city of the killing soul
Whose holes multiply by the one
Ignorant of ONÖNYXA's gone calculating flux
EKSTONISTIAN's cataracted copse
Her forest floor moving beyond its composed
Self within oxygenated Earth even now.

In blood sacrifice
The Fifth World's promise
Houses but one    will be burnt will demolish
and so by the sweet singing
rushing shore
Immense as its vision    rushing thru the floor
Sacrifices more    immense by endentured durance
Willingly    drunk in the salination
The shoreline's window a breaking hyaline
soporific rebellion.
Spirits    light as smoke    fade
Power will not deny Daemonic SHIRU
Whose essence is an age of ZAS
Nor the compelling path of ONÖNYXA
Whose sister EKSTONISTIAN
Mirrors all the sources of illumination.
Thus has PLNIPLOI been placed on all planes
To extract the rituals or source-code to war
Blight and blood be given
In its needful guise
The Universal composition of Will as Power.
In his Being's name in titanic insignificance
An office held    and not a house be left to stand
yet will SHIRU sense his memory
Tethered to that state by this emblem
Within the staging realms of no thought.
Thus all stories tell the Fifth World
The future self
Whose spacious domains remain
no ecstatic
To those who battle in the vein of human sources.
Its right to rule there usurped
By true turmoil which births
Song's reproductive parsing ration
Determines the work's direction.

## nineteenth sketch]

the center-space at the crest of the stellar ovoid wave and out of the light the embodiment the locomotility of SHIRU singing distances and directions interstitial might of AHNÁHR'S land all of it made plain laid bare made to mirror the immensity of the northern martial constellations burning brightly in the cold night within the OURANIAN heights....... .

## twentieth sketch]

and this skull-shell contested and questioned and brought about in a coitus or maieutic within incubating reproductive cellular activity his circle is perfect his plane has no ridges no morphology to speak of dwells

thus the stakes were raised and SHIRU was brought into the world to seduce and then release the inhabitants of Earth within the jointure of east and west where the arbitrary capacity of all language resides

theologies likewise have the breath of their own language and communicate or could fall in love with all other theologies their diaphragms are listed in the UNESCO book of extinct or nearly extinct species

the Aztec's Fifth World was a prophecy heard in the meat of our slumbering American spaces systolic diastolic paleozoic spunk

death's heads passing over into incubation at the center-space of the world the emblematic seizure in the ovoid cave work unites the worlds the two eggs in overlap OÖND and OOM

within and without the contending and inter-animating forces of animal and sentient man the gods AHNÁHR and SHIRU and PLNIPLOI ONÖNYXA EKSTÖNISTIAN and ZAS others yet to be brought forth grow toward the prophetic character rumor has while arms and limbs couple and soothe one another in the knowledge of pure being by words that form anatomy's reaching doing gripping and

the Mind of Man PLNIPLOI who has made his way thru faint signal to usurp the thin thread of Being within the eggs the forces of inter-play jealously seizes the path THERSEYN found by the zone of gestation

## MAGNETIZATION RADIATION FRUCTIFICATION

What is this child of the world
Gathering sense within his wave-like singing?
Were I not the evolution of the universal plain of eternity
I could have continued without his shape calling to my center.
But now where is my center what is the length of time?
A small moon's half-light
rocks me into galactic formation
and every worship becomes a new arbitrary theology.

Why was I left to this device
and from what interstice unknown yet Earthly
Such singing emanates plastic irradiate
Assuming my own large length.
Have I been tricked
lulled
incorporated?

SHIRU speaks thence stopping his song:
*What immense power you possess in the world of Earth*
*Long and big a muscular cloud*
*sweating over my brain's bed.*

*I am urging you above the precessional*
*The axis-tree's tapered mouth in eternity*
*Newly formed within evolutionary living.*

*I have only wanted to attend your existence.*
*And this the seductive songs allude*
*is not your only self*
*But called by your own*

*At the center-space of this very same song*
*Drilling my breath it*
*took my heart away.*

*A new age begins    all eyes wake to this urge*
*Further heard in the dense copse of EKSTONISTIAN*
*Wakes to the form of song itself.*

The chest as a cloud of AHNÁHR's body
Descended over the aether and rode
Into this troubled time    the ovoid center-space
Immense    his new-found shape.

Together    SHIRU and AHNÁHR

come into the Earth.

Radiation waved thruout the Earth

and out    to Galactic Empyreans.

## twenty first sketch]

a contention and controversy by the plasticity by the body's new rendition which sings shoots at what it aimed for an incursion from the width of the planet     lattitudes which name our center-space consistently below the waist and stand for what

thought
  once
    was

## The cavernous source

*Your might is not complete* sings SHIRU
*Within the expanding worldhood of man*
*Within these desolate mountains*

*snowy cloudy shelves and shores and*
*sky-scapes of the Ouranian…… .*

*You have been made by the presence of love*
*Thus has the lonely hour captured imagination*
*and formed within the eternal*

*so now the way into Earth opens and beckons intention*

*it is your contentious loud turbulent return.*

# Processing the World-Tree

# Part 4

*a combinatory helixing Daemon the mind now symbolic movement thru an image composed within and without*

*so behold the new memories of the State of Man*

*behold the Stages in rendezvous*

*an evolutionary meridian deep within the body the universe its contours deepened thru each figure's formation now the World-Eggs hatch*

deep

within caves and crevices deep within holistic openings OKEANOS willed the Daughters of AHNÁHR send and sow to edges of the World the shape of OKEANOS nacreous purpling shades representing realms of night and day surging contracting labor of all who mount the crystal sea sends to the bottoms of loam and loess searching Earth's braided rivers distilled water to feed seedings an entire species' contention their surrender in the vegetable to witness the protean dynamic

from her view MOIRA salutes her workers within the growing emanation of the populated clouds *immortality we've built for that I salute you and reel my privates toward yours there take a load off!*

and so it begins to rain reactionary measure held in the momentary exposure of the marble's pudenda whose shape's a mound of meat memorializing scavenging ages long past done but looming in the world's contended time

petty and vain realizations will not plumb intersticted Galactic realms where SHŌÖNWU prepares his charge with AHNÁHR in a certain and neverending battle over absolute nothingness within mosaic of the living shelf of stars germinating molecular position in pre- and post-verbal extremities sound and light to thus cozzen man before and after he begins

EKSTONISTIAN now begins her rise into the OURANIAN

there was in the brain of Man but the arrival of THERSEYN blowing winds from this Book thru the Daughters spreading with them to undo duration of nature as the superstructure thus mount verbal dexterity in re-doubled ecstatic singing where his world reflecting worlds are mirrored by the flaw of constellated ecliptic meridian magnetics and precession-like activations the distance of image to object

THERSEYN yawps up and out to the OURANIAN and in that moment there is born the rumor EKSTONISTIAN may indeed be THERSEYN *this whole scene is so freaking gone must I now become the immensity of all dream-time pressing toward what? the necessities which haunt all the Paleo with re-atomization to one day build tiny names given by both the mindless and the minding?*

emblematic alarm living pulse from Man beast and gaseous letters of ZAS but the Book of AHNÁHR as he contends with absolutely nothing paused for re-positioning the Mansion of SHŌÖNWU the eternal splurge as it has doubled in force for this new age gathering light and dark the World-Tree whose blown-up consecration begins from the Daughters fingers working the knapping stone gathering waves in the caves just below the table-top Earth

OURANIAN time by virtue of all precessionary activity within and without the Earth so in plenitude of all the Earth's round movement wobbling circle seeks perfect the human species thru a 26,000 year cycle now within half-life countdown mathematicals known to human-kind since the beginning will be thus undone

every single day another 26,000 year axial enscription completely traversed pivotal to the axial age moving in a 1,000 year parameter to grow a doubling dynamic intellectual promethean epimethean age like never before

AHNÁHR rides down to survey the World tho his eye in the OURANIAN merges the thrumming fingers the Daughters spectral tissues the doubled light and dark the World-Tree now far into eternity THERSEYN captures and stills by coming to time there another moment the edge of the World cries a triumphant living insurgence echoes everything within one diction the human entered the center of his evolution

*ageless rebellion stirs within the Earth stirs within starry depths stirs within non-existent center of all non-existent perfection the existence of which recalls her gone shape her long gone shape the age of long gone figures the contours the World's productive capacities in a re-productive age*

walls geometries the human mind working fingers of the Daughters alight and darken from OKEANOS and channel the Axis-Tree branching in and out up and down the length of precessional time

Daughters plunge into work with abandon spirits souls emanations of ancestral unconscious desire a necessitous pump in catapultation the essence of Oceanic splurge out from the edge of OKEANOS AHNÁHR now up into the channel which begins to funnel upward spinning plying shooting emblazoning dusk and dawn thrumming from epochs great and small into the new Axis-Tree wobbling World the constellated differential of matter and creation precession of the World-Tree

ZAS thru temper of the moment there was a moment within all faces as bombardment halted into the World leapt his features length of every body animal anthropomorphic industrial and then made way to the marble bed of MOIRA

in the meanwhile this moment also ushered the Paleo toward center THERSEYN occupies merely as a holding pattern to catch the evolutionary intellect by dialectical former selves

AHNÁHR sends his own specter toward the constellated might toward his martial place within SHŌÖNWU and shatters the bowl of sky above OKEANOS with a black and interstitial branch or limb of precessional empty universal fourfold position an erection never before witnessed by any age within human memory

MOIRA forms an eclipse above the Daughters *out from my womb the issue of an entire world a new generation of giant proportion no more will I see a flock of bleating lost and mewling kids in a wilderness of mind! movement I command cease from this whirling upward toward center a position I did not request!*

a glistening slug deposits spittle upon the screen of night and makes its way within the new time it will be known as the space of unending and the vegetable the garden thence a tamed wild now enters the poetry the calendars and the moon's light also split between was and is … … …

Daughters of AHNÁHR unleash the burthen of continual work from finger to wave-sound to emblematic charge and display the rod or missile launched toward Axis-Tree its canopy's height's measured distance of time from solar time night's time to wheeling hub sidereal constellations layered in ever-enduring distance traveling precessional new clock unending unknowable real contingent palpable and unconcealing thru temporal folds its erection for the destined OURANIAN folds

so the World-Tree's axis contains THERSEYN who now begins in search of EKSTONISTIAN whose Forest became essential nature to all the world's signatures symbolic wonders a Forest of consciousness a wilderness of unconscious untended time

the Axis-Tree the alpha delta sidereal time the time of AHNÁHR Earthly time connexion of all error endeavor eternal differential wobbling rotation Earth raptures within ecstatic bodies real imagined gorgeous eyelids Oceanic holistic beginning dates a recessive domain spells the World not with sleep waning mental energy but glancings a moving pleasure-inducing body of work yet to be entered

so now PLNIPLOI contrary to the precession the Axis-Tree grows within four-fold illusion a plastic embodiment all true judgment … … …

sweeping eternal bombardment's of the Axis-Tree the erection of destiny catapulted toward the World-Tree in raiment of green explosive inevitabilities EKSTONISTIAN achieves flight above OKEANOS the whirling encircling helix of Axis and Tree

dead specter never before emanated within the time of Earth makes its way toward Daughters' busy fingers and up toward immense OURANIAN bombardment AHNÁHR a distance within precession of the planet knows thru THERSEYN's attachment to EKSTONISTIAN within contours of Time and Space

death's informed all nature all the World time denied from solar to constellated universal *is* the life of THERSEYN everything in an outlay the temporal fold grows from Plains up in order to die in the sprouting place

Daughters continue their work from fingers thru network of cave complex yet knapped walls rock flaking to sharp nodules cutting weapons the very round of all symbolic uses the material world but in this moment wet liminal as explosions continue above the edge the world of Earth

bombarded length duration expanding Axis-Tree wobbling eternally loaded constellation AHNÁHR a martial mansion within the empty reaches of the northern OURANIAN curve a seeming end so dark the position therein doesn't matter it's the sound the snake making out the slow crawl of the tortoise's shell

MOIRA does not believe the truth of the World fled so holds her marble couch the hours tick within marbled halls

the Four Directions of the World come to the Daughters' care fevered attentions rise in sound emanating intelligence shapes and figures toward bombardment the World-Tree the center of Earth up and out to stellar bounds an eternally measuring ejaculation of time

damage to the World is complete and PLNIPLOI arrives beheading bodies from souls as if he will now own every moment to come from the silent forms and figures

THERSEYN weeps at this beheading proving his own existence a generation begun in the bowels of terror by bodies of a billion located sleeping still-born so he dives up catches hold of the limbs the World-Tree gasping finally spent he is

Daughters at OKEANOS whip up the great arrival releasing ZAS and MOIRA toward upper reaches enbrainéd yet the sounding of the crystal sea all within the World the Earth now rocks rumors crash one to another becoming one then another becoming combining without use of any mental constraint so PLNIPLOI ushers the ancient world the meso-near and the Paleo distant the will to murder ritual work toward sacrifice

ZAS into sight the entire World shows visions the female tendering every wish so the lock within time and space industrial consciousness now networking taboo

PLNIPLOI grows to this State of Contention whereby opposites congeal no longer wobble or flow the essence in fuel chambers soul's engine belly brow gargantuan repose signal hatred the base industrial dynamic spectral emanations at the well-springs holistic sources of OKEANOS PLNIPLOI ends in sophistication of the Paleo

OKEANOS within vast deep crevices of Earth falls toward emblematic catapultation up toward spectral re-animation into the subjective Axis-Tree whose eternal formality regulates calls forth every dead matter to join in the living material evolutions

you will interpret as you've always done right at the very edge moments as they become known not a moment before or after exactly there it appears to you to belong and let loose toward another 26,000 year cycle

ZAS unfurls his arms of gaseous length about the future murdering infant son carries him to the bed-chamber of MOIRA a teeming World of noise and error suckles his thought determining edges of eternity his sacrificial reign begins

Daughters thrum and turn and the waves of Ocean crash emblazoned explosions in releasement of form and shape contour time extending solar time so they sing *keep it lit and moving toward constellated eternal difference now sling we the image of fingers five times two into the World's contour an Axis-Tree loaded with meridian light an endless distance yet to explore by the protean conception the apotheosis of OKEANOS*

MOIRA moves thru dream-vision wondering why aesthetic stages never bothered her before the voices within melodies the backward descant the arrival of AHNÁHR interpreted as the sweet essence of reproductive and re-generational thrall her own the objective correlative won't understand

PLNIPLOI secures intellectual industry networking a murder thru thoughtless bloody judgment beheading eternal opposition to periplus man's first instinct travel and observe far into pleasure forms before and after any time he otherwise thought

THERSEYN peers down the gloomy time the new age the tired human relic laboring under vast composite destruction of PLNIPLOI now to become every center *mother and father send into industrial cold the absolute tyrant mind shape even after their coupling delivers eternal spectral images into evolution the universal view the sidereal meridian ignored this new shape the World-Tree a non-rotation or circulation of investment all I were ever waiting for* twenty second sketch]

centerspace of the ovoids in overlap

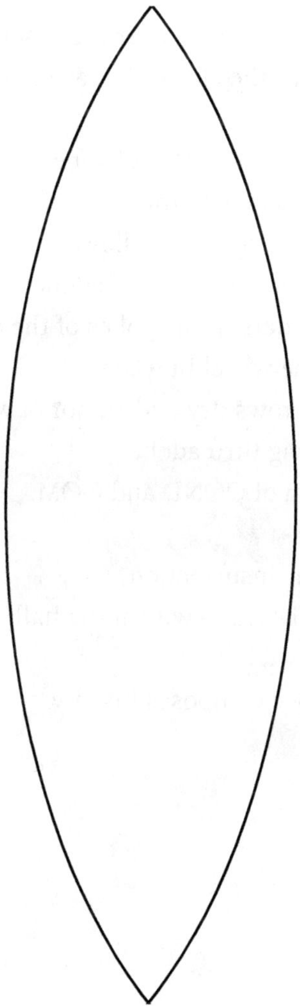

## TIME THE EVOLUTION OF THE MESO-NEAR

The Daemonix in periplum
And yet does QAPTAKUSS rule his hall
Pissed by the disappearance of ONÖNYXA.

Can you not feel time over the desert
Loping coyote or the claws of a ravenous hawk?

The Fifth World lives in his clamped sight
And memory reads the prophetic Fifth World
nowhere is blood made to flow.
He rules from expanses of adobe
issuing orders from spokes of the everyday.
Now the wheel in water
Stops the furrows dry and rumor of water
Bellies clamoring thru adobe
Toward horizon of OÖND and OOM.

Cellular insurrection
Maddens QAPTAKUSS within the hall.

A deathly silence composes his city.

SHIRU with music        lifts them
Becomes the returning apparition of ONÖNYXA
Flying from horizon of the world
Answering their very work

    while EKSTONISTIAN's influence

Grows branches to the Meso-near.
    Her pregnant belly full of wonder
Prophets and priests expire from revelation
Working toward food instead of starvation at the Paleo-far.

## twenty third sketch]

thus has the metaphysical been delivered dead to the table     or rather completely mundane yet not dead here rather the *Ontic* semantical wave has become a split infinitive
          charming the     no not charm not by any simple application of grace     rather the metaphysic as a value has been handed to the wave or stream of seduction     and by this primary relation the entire world is given a life and death dance whose macabre     whose also leafy verdant feature holds and puts forth a stem     what former reason     what former logical World     or age or place     once held

          running out now thru top and bottom both     World as song upon which shadow AHNÁHR once inhabited draws near to all bodies thus invades their spirits     men and women alike     tended to by gender neutral SHIRU     thus engendered SHIRU
   master initiator of enstaged states

## World-eggs

SHIRU my new teacher
Primitive neo-wave being's rationate
Hold me for I'm fear
And truth our mighty existence
Edges accomplices toward what we mean
Ouranian development
Being Knowledge Writing

*Writing* : the center-space overlap.

THERSEYN uncovers his own infant nature now
In the covering of EKSTONISTIAN's forest
Lost his corporeality looms
From one bone one occipital and one
Shiver of immense doubt.

The Ouranian's lost! Dark
hands I see reaching

can these anatomical parts
spring from lips?
or are they meant for dirt alone?

What vision of what memory?
I who created heaven within galactic awe
Stand before crowded stupid depths of your world
Hungering stretching imagination by its own mortality
By its categories : the anatomies of an extinction!
All's in complete collapse!
How can anything that exists be known by the soul?
I've been a body thru your lips and mind
By the attachment SHIRU and the Ouranian

Ovoid forms obtain
    yet nothing I would order to sight
        re-sounds without the sheerness of power
            colossal eye-slit of a holed-in shadowy species.

This IS the whole mighty world then
Believed to be the very essence of shade
Traveling thru what was and thru what is
Contending within the physical body
An existence trampled    ruined by stupidity's metaphysic
Daemonic short-sightedness
The human realm……… . .

SHIRU
floats over the bodies of men and women
And comes to the inchoate wavering silhouette of AHNÁHR:
*Trouble yourself with nothing*
*The seduction of the world is wakening*
*To the orders you once possessed in the Universal.*
*It is nothing but the existence of a species*
*Within a genus attached to the underside of Ourania*
*Having left their stations within one Daemonic*
*For procreation of their bodies within that body*
*Re-establishes    invigorates the true root.*
*Before the Daemonic*
*These bodies were of one compact*
*Now to become one again you've come*
*To me and I to you to be.*
*Destruction of this species comes from my song*
*And the music will not end*
*until they feel my triumphant flesh*
*released into their vacuity*
*thus enabling eternity within*
*turning back the tide of their ignorant mind*

*souls sent up into AHNÁHR's descending feature*
*from this new distance*
*this new dimension of silence.*

SHIRU
spoke as in a trance to suck AHNÁHR into
Soul-space song's overlap gap in flesh which
Holds the ages by evolutionary concentration.
And from the back-side of all time
dense space empties the World-Eggs
sighs to the voices which now inhale
center-space of the ovoid overlap.

In lambent folds of flesh
AHNÁHR'S head flooded eternal progression
Vanishing
yet-to-be-written verses of existence.

Is man's fate so simple
That he has never known nor witnessed these two chambers?
The world's ended by this ignorance
And knowledge has a double-beat beginning and an end
Thru one atmospheric regulation the eye-slit
Yearning spell which seems expire forever
Yet retreats toward destiny by this shore
Inspiring holistic multitudes.

*Is this finality?* AHNÁHR bellows
As if he has to recalculate the soul.

SHIRU'S lips
played the first music
And approaches the lambent bodies
Suspiring in their own unknown orgy.

He enters each as they then see
The form the beat the stress then the spell
World-Eggs synthesizing all existence
By destiny of living creation
Beyond civilizations beyond holistic worshippers
Who were their elders sapience
lost by that emptiness.

The signal permeates
Stopping those souls forming in shadow
PLNIPLOI'S signal alone could only accomplish
Thru dark fealty to an inept knowledge
Death-strain thru usufructating greed.

Why has PLNIPLOI such a reach within the nature of mankind?

*He was born from the mind as a machinery of man*
*A deep desire to erase the written glimpse of each breath*
*And replace himself as the calculating distance of destiny.*

SHIRU
hums and floats thru a scansion of bodies
And at last reaches the vast anatomy of the fucking Gods
reaching to soothe the features of ONÖNYXA
urging her further from Daemonic parents
to couple now with him by the World-Eggs.

SHIRU
penetrates her flesh
Diving into her field
And flowering to apex of the center-space
To tease out sense-apprehension a wheel of petals
Nearly breathless held in contention
From nearly the first moment of life itself.

Soaring thru short and unconscious sighs
Each new-borne soul's re-coupled
By Daemonic leaves of a green book
  whose writing's mirrored in the fall from flight
  whose center's within the other's imprint
            so expressed.

PLNIPLOI
  hears news of the fresh souls
Delivers from his own anatomical assumption
Emanation thru space-time a rendition of mind
Permeating cortices of the World-Eggs
Stalling the new-borne rite within our overlap
Separations and de-couplings toward darkness
Procreative contention from West to East
North to South   re-usurpationing winds begin
Who steal a portion of the future
Concealing the future   encoding the future
Memorized thru this forgetful exegesis of PLNIPLOI.

O
*sweet*   ONÖNYXA sighs.
*SHIRU*
*imaginative immensities*
*my song as close as if yours*
*make me one   again*
*let me know......*

SHIRU's imagination
  speaks thru the music :
    *Come   to the other side of this place.*

Eyes open within the writhing anatomical
Mouths open to the solidifying oxygen
  closed by the joy-gush glimpse expressing
      waves of release
  up thru warmth in frozen atmosphere of time
Sweating procreative meal at the edge of all knowledge

    ONÖNYXA    SHIRU
    nacreous extinctions
    reified animalcules and populations….. . .

Thought    shoots thru AHNÁHR
As the sight and soon limbs of ONÖNYXA
Her magnificent head
    by the rime of after-thought.

Breath-loss ceases    the wavering ceases
AHNÁHR rises above ONÖNYXA
Straight thru her crystallizing dimension
Refracting cold air by his warming soul
Melting her body's glance in a multitude of
Overlapping  ovoidal  visions.

Souls of the World-Eggs rise and shudder
Moving toward the warm center-space
Overlapping icicles at the ends of shortened breath
Anatomizing love by tens of thousands of glancings
Hundreds of thousands of glimpsings.

        SHIRU
    would have for eternity
Coupling warm species in a genus of the World-Eggs
And for all time release man's nature
Toward imagination of the reproductive

So that bodies begin again a slow agglomeration
A steady evolution toward the center-space.

*OOM once quivered with OÖND.*
*ONÖNYXA once was wakened and wandered.*
*Existence quivers and releases itself*
*Into the ovoid overlap*
*center-space of time.*

PLNIPLOI's repelled in the sound of their will-to-power.

SHIRU's music
glides among bodies
Making each the anatomy of the World-Eggs
Telling time the image
of EKSTONISTIAN :

*a copse expressed from the eye-slit*
*Multiplies and a forest emerges*
*And so one skull's exhumed*
*thru iterations of one anatomic.*

## twenty fourth sketch]

it is just a glimpse and it was just a glance sketched out the work all mankind is now consumed by

scenes of *La Venta* the basalt altar roped round umbilically both birth and death sacrifice and symbol scenes of *Teotihuacan* the steps up to the central platform and stoned altar-piece scenes of the *Cahokia* the buried alive frozen in the sacrifice scenes of *Moula-Guercy* further back into the paleo the slaughter for food which turns on its own the primary mode thence replaced by symbolic offerings an age beholden to the madness of an empty belly archaic by its arch in our time a rope or cord wrapping all around

*scenes now of wakjąka of the northern* Hočąk

*wakjąka dancing with the ducks he's out of his mind and talks to the ducks and shows them all his dances and then the ducks begin to speak to him but he's the true clown and there will be no other wakjąka*

*he's actually quite pissed and into the four directions as far as he can see he stops singing this goes on for the time of the deer constellation until the fox when the clown goes to sleep when wakjąka goes to sleep in front of his fire where he was roasting his great haul and catch the foxes come near and they hear and then smell something gas powering out of the clown's asshole wakjąka is so pleased and fat from his meal and from the stopping up of the singing that his gut is speaking out of his ass and his face is sleeping and smiling in the pleasing sated glut an entire nation sleeping in the stopped up guts speaking to the foxes wakjąka has made the farts very expressive and so the foxes steal all the food from the ashes in the fire it is very good so they bring some more meat back to the ashes and when wakjąka wakes up he hears his ass making a new language but he thinks it's the ducks who are clowning around with his meal so he gets angry and decides to get even with the ducks grabs some of the ashes burning in the fire and puts it to his asshole to shut it up and burns himself ululating it's heard everywhere and the foxes are already over by the place where the two rivers meet have gone under the hill but the clown wakjąka isn't satisfied with how he's stopped up his ass so he gives it another go and mushes the flesh into place but it's not perfect will have to do it's all wrinkled the flesh is but he had to stop it but as he's now walking along he sees that some other hunter was out in the woods or must have been because some meat fat was there by the tree     so wakjąka went up to the piece of fat and smelled it and ate it and it tasted pretty good     there was actually another piece as well wakjąka went and found the trail the hunter had let fall from his hunting sack it must have been pretty good actually darn good meatfat*

*but then the clown wakjąka notices he is back at the pond in the woods where the Hočąk used to hunt and sees his old fire and ashes*

*and there also his guts because he has gotten messy with the ashes to his asshole trying to stop it from singing     all of his guts and those are his guts that he had followed from the     from all the way around and around it must have been a time     eating his gut-fat which he finds very tasty     borders himself into where his nation was for a time     meanwhile the foxes have tails of white twinkle gone into the ground*

## twenty fifth sketch]

democracy is a waste of time    industry a waste of space    together they speak as if they knew    and the world exists in a timeless belt around them both    a bolt of cloth or lightning    accessed by song

when will the overlap dawn    when will it symbolize and thru extinction pull stars out of the real nightsky?

## twenty sixth sketch]

if *homo sapiens* think they can continue without a size change then they simply haven't been paying attention thru-out actual time

these specimens these bones these findings        unearthings

        scale a period of gestational conception and inception        and leave as they enter
by fore-head or fore-armed positions within and without     an eternal coupling by their overlap

## twenty seventh sketch]

a dance      within the copse      eyepiecebranch

cataract      trees in time multiply      from the one tree a small seed a tiny blotch fallen from the air occludes the previous

and tho no one singing's heard    tho the world has come to an end

it is for her dance in the smallest forest    copse of her eye    cataract
holds the never-given-out note
THERSEYN gathers

to one day!

cover Earth      cover as by protein Sun

the bone-white milk-music

## MOIRA

*I am the hour of the world's time*
*Counting waves that sound*
*Within cowardly shell of the world's prison*
*Will know this puissant pleasure*

*Power*

*Come to my willing and dark son*

*PLNIPLOI*

*with gifts preternatural*
*Beyond even those who worship and tow*
*My name's obsession ZAS*

*into firmament of a new age.*

## twenty eighth sketch]

**θήρ** used without vowel tones in a declension which operates thru consonance to formalize a multitude of localities within "deed"

**there** a transmigration of worlds poised to seize the anatomy of the world within each prolapsed tone funeral speech and thus the song's score

as the animal is a *ther*iomorphic agglomeration to human dimension **their** mere obsession turns to marble

and composition suffers

from a pre-biotic series of shapes and identities we re-atone or lope at

an age an empire of laval con-ceiling influenza

to inure a focus for the holistically consumed discarded non-constellational

# Processing the World-Tree

# Part 5

*try to explain PLNIPLOI you end up sounding like THERSEYN try to explain THERSEYN you end up helping PLNIPLOI shut the Daemonic down*

why

does man believe THERSEYN to have died when he inhabits the ever re-created existence conjugated from OURANIAN anatomies

man's emptied by the Daemon PLNIPLOI!

the Axis-Tree displays a multitude in fact everything makes way thru the funneling wind

mankind has no recourse no solution but re-birth haunted and urged by that glowing objective born inter-glacial at the edge of the Northern Boreal an age of both artefact and controversy every acting Daemon now vies for human eyes

THERSEYN a progression of event forever free goaded from AHNÁHR OURANIA branching potentially and in actuality toward a well within SHŌÖNWU watery yet starry in pin-pricks of martial defensive offensive darklight

AHNÁHR the umbellical the architectonic OURANIAN element receives the Daughter's sighs the funnel of wind spectering channel of axial work thrumming to the World-Tree's exploding loose load of green and white sap guards the walls the passageways of running meridian light blank dark by which a language preserved at one end the mansion a tortoise by the other in material radioactivities snake whose head's in form and formality the form of an egg

vision bombardment consecration World-Tree wobbling pivot planetary specters toward inter-stellar magnetism universal temporality precessional contouring activity moving within moving without trance the matter contentious to emblem and image

..................

AHNÁHR took EKSTONISTIAN so mankind might see THERSEYN and offered precession of the World-Tree as passage into her

PLNIPLOI was conceived within the industry of MOIRA killed our path toward the World-Tree so we delve toward THERSEYN's time in this dark time and write a Book the resurrection of EKSTONISTIAN beyond contemporary measure a protozoaelogical seduction the archaeology of aesthetic and industry to transliterate any difference time has from its own malformed dis-intuited selves

..................

PLNIPLOI speaks *what are these rumors of emanation there never was and never will be conflagration of spirit all's within the time my birth an objective I push or pull alone to find interpretation wear it end of story enough already*

PLNIPLOI's followers mark as Law the Being of an entire species deny to THERSEYN omniscient death and life

an axonic dendritic rhetoric an objective scientific quasi-empirical subjected to its own as a possessive feature within all matter within all scenes and times within the very full feature of a narkoaesthetical inheritance

..................

the exit completely closed but for those sucked to the channel up into the funneling World-Tree

..................

PLNIPLOI dares THERSEYN forth from the World-Tree an opposition deepening ignorance time become his way of making it to the new age

his distribution of self-expansion the mind a channel now in self erasure placing himself at center to pursue THERSEYN his process erasing precessional activated seeds stems now into superstructure eternal time supernatural injection seeking Axial Age seeking every form of self or seeming

explosions burst from the canopy the World-Tree above OKEANOS he sees as if below adrift in the interstitial then more catapultations right above his head turns to see his difference in the funneling whirling time-channel so he nods off wish-fulfilling back into supernatural time before this sucking upsurge from OKEANOS the World-Tree the vacuuming mansion in the Northern OURANIAN

.................

Daughters fling beyond the World's edge the firmament the heavenly precession of emanation THERSEYN surrounded by green spirit EKSTONISTIAN whose eyes over hills after endless Plains of Earth run toward rivers returning toward oceanic upward distillation

thru forests of memory tympanum-burst thru emblematic thrumming fingers light and dark sparking on flint in the knapping of the Paleo-stone throes of appreciation contours the human animal a World-Soul hovers within and without

PLNIPLOI is its champion who could have predicted this or get around this Fifth World it has stolen all prophecy all meaning all phenomenology to the Meso-near and so we get THERSEYN only within the Axis-Tree delineated by Daughters of AHNÁHR their thrumming hands and fingers meditating working toward conflagration of the wobbling Earthly endeavor under the umbel the watchful purpose of AHNÁHR's coordination thru time and EKSTONISTIAN as she alone holds to the Paleo-far

.................

an entire world over again our only hope to avoid this terrible nightmare this ignorant PLNIPLOI who cannot see he's destined for the World-Tree too and as the age musters forth its oldest positions within and without hell-bent to annihilate intuitive auscultations an osculating propinquity too much for hatred's bed its altar of basalt preserved in *La Venta* shows the still-born jaguar god limp offering out of the stone-age the pretense of its build laborious workmanship thus the image the form and content of a perfect death

.................

to spin his body as if it were a blade beheading the living specters make their way toward the Axis-Tree limbs severed the blood sacrifice wailing time his influence to grip the many willingly accept PLNIPLOI so the calendar carried by individuals bands of individuals come gather pray offer themselves the green countries sacrifice this hemisphere PLNIPLOI demands and under the blade go the heads each from his State glowing indifference hammering Law to universal morality dismissing aesthetic connexions to the phanozoic

PLNIPLOI goads the human animal from temporal lobe the empirical shutdown occurs within finitude of man's meat never to gain access to precessional polemics the cognitive resonance within a turnip say where the protean forms in organismal display an entire living spirit's been made to correspond to disguises of marbled meat in an allegory of the mind of PLNIPLOI

..................

THERSEYN grew to become a language and out of the letters connexion with the galactic maw inter-stellar meridian destroyed pretended Being projected by ZAS and his followers SEVLESMEHT MOIRA especially who turned away and could not face his activations from the endless depths of time and space

toward OURANIAN canopy ejaculating in open endless space spectral onrush the upper reaches of the World just below the funneling winds from OKEANOS the supernatural superstructure the gods have also been erased forgotten the State of Man brought PLNIPLOI whose ignorance entrusts systems and distribution networks ignorant objectivities without opposition from existence all now in semblance to the image of machinery simple to complex morphing sight away from its biological form thus the industrial come to its logical conclusion

..................

first the Daughters blended with the work this was even long after knapping flinting catapultation as an artistic industry invented reproduced took for ZAS his emblematic scenery added the rod the shaft the spear up out over the edge of OKEANOS thus OKEANOS came into Being the lashing fretful World raging Oceanic clashes phenomenal contentions the endless planetary its universal stretch up to the Plains of table-top Earth came and stole the Daughters yet they continued to work but a naked brilliance made them throw their hands in air it was as if the desires of EKSTONISTIAN came to their work suddenly re-defining ancient art and work in a starry immensity up above

PLNIPLOI were he not born from ZAS and MOIRA throw up hands or extend arms from elbow to finger-joint reflexivity toward upper realms even the Plains of Earth or in real ambition toward the green canopy whirling emanating living dead souls sucked to it the Axis-Tree which wobbles for the planetary universal precession the Daughters of AHNÁHR their fingers extending meridian knuckles of light in homage to EKSTONISTIAN the bombardment above OKEANOS would continue thru funneling World-Tree in the pivot of the bed of the planet

..................

THERSEYN runs to the green raiment of the World-Tree envisioning triumphs the natural world held within it to prove the interindependence of all things the Axis-Tree perpetuates integrity within swelling precession AHNÁHR's temporal lode his head bows sighs yet rises absorbing activity OURANIAN light that martial position within the Mansion not of the mind but meridian contour time the pleasure to thwart the symbolic misuse or disuse toward war and sacrificial slaughter thus an early influence to Epicurus his Axial understanding the atomic that some atoms must swerve and fall to avoid the entire symbolic lust otherwise existence gives itself too prematurely and thus do all minds or souls and so thus we have a blown-up World-Tree

..................

PLNIPLOI's never wrong THERSEYN's always failing distanced and eternalized to one another by expanding universals and AHNÁHR then become an empirical formulation now to be the center to covet

..................

EKSTONISTIAN whose spectral emanation goads the World-Tree to bloom in crazy bursts wet with light eternal conflagration and the willing *Was* of THERSEYN a diction *and* attribute within the Book of Time and Space

history now the impenitent horizon of PLNIPLOI man's high and mighty mammon toward his low and deaf realm doubt also surety alongside the feminine shade have crossed one to each other to realize the unconscious drift by which tragedy an entire species

.................

emanating thru temporal lode AHNÁHR whose blasted OURANIAN distance passes from body to body shared living eternal rooms in the mansion of SHŌÖNWU pressing thru martial array slow Tortoise in disguise the protection of Earth surrounded by interstitial repose and quick ejaculating head of the Snake

... ... *am I only human in non-human form there where my being's shot into?* ...

THERSEYN leaps once again thru the precessional Axis-Tree spectral emanation the final brain up toward the martial protection the Northern Mansion hiding in the open while the symbolic continues to be ballistic contanment in unconscious seduction toward war and accumulation for the former

.................

PLNIPLOI typing on the writing machine in white light and heat all the while tapping fingers the Daughters throw into their own shape the keys above OKEANOS the explosive keys combining all not yet injected back to PLNIPLOI's narkoaesthesia an art hidden in symbolic drift from age to age a seed for war and baseless sacrifice

mankind evolved toward OKEANOS now blinded by limited PLNIPLOI angered first by the industry at OKEANOS beyond any sense or reason but that manifest thru beheading murder the human form proceeds from inward self to all contingent outer thru blinding white heat networks the body's blades beheading the newly sacrificial human

..................

the World-Tree

in periploi thru universal martial position AHNÁHR's risen magnetic lode-pole and meridian mansion

so we witness the coming bombardment the lost found figure of Man THERSEYN within Axis-Tree flowing wobbling toward its destiny lifts his voice and body the OURANIAN contours echoing where he leaps to sight dis

*charging*
*voilàs!*

## twenty ninth sketch]

now to the final giving-up-the-ghost      soul-spunk

and the world holds for one-day

nation contending in a long-term there as allure and glammar and so seduction of all naming

the *objet de trope*

air

so small moment
poverty
material helix
architects
prison-cells
numbered

dust to atomic

proto-biotic

head

## thirtieth sketch]

mind will have nothing to do with him and SEVLESMEHT takes this position in the "world" now as a learner or shaman politician following orders set into place by the mirror seeing a metaphysical charge might build in a network of ownership
thus he begins to find a way thru and beyond even his own smoke-hole

we say do not speak until sufficient reason a quantum sufficient for there to be reason a reasoning of sufficiency

there must be a well within full embodiment for belief to erect itself and so the self poses this dilemma

posturing stretching into and out of

EKSTONISTIAN
trembles at the re-staging of all thought for her statement already leafed thru

## EKSTONISTIAN's GREEN MOMENT

SHIRU's an apparition at these windows
Borne on immense cracked time
Melted from the sands of time
A circle a circumference he calls.

EKSTONISTIAN's body is this window
SHIRU's given her by seeming infinity
A World-Tree to reach
                    and touch

*and the momentary e-merges     universal.*

The State of Man's in overlap
As she shakes the tree
Center-spaces of the World-Eggs
Scatter to four directions
Spreading rumor will one day spell
Apparition as atomic reality
Origin replacing origin

the bodily placement of an infinite art.

So our call expands
Shrunk to the FAERYS order
As in a staged and unreal dilemma
Of wood and leaf in a small corner copse where
EKSTONISTIAN dreams her forest into view.

Now
from Being immense she shouts :
*Daemon of the known world!*
*Send me the lover of this grove.*
*Everything has changed*

*The world goes on without me*
*yet only by art I'm to live*
*Who left the dead history and place of many holes*
*Defiant afraid trembling in one green river*
*Pooled here by*
*nowhere's news one hole alone to please.…. . .*

Voices of the world
Whether in harmony or confusion
Eternal progressions
Cease.
SHIRU now occupies
Center of EKSTONISTIAN's eye
Gathering above her pool's clear glass
Descending to the floor
from canopied height
Waving in sound a series
Tones composed to be as bone.

EKSTONISTIAN trembles at the sight
A skull whose slender solid state
Appears to grow or
Settling into the pool-side
Grows green with this place of changes
Seeming opposite to white substance
planted in a garden the wide Earth over.

SHIRU advances
From call she shook at the tree
From memory THERSEYN has
Within human fold skull-bone
By which her place in him's begun erect.

*Only a creature meant to match*
*Existence itself*      *infinite in variety*
*Yet finite touch*
*For me to reach and.…. .*

His voice
standing before
Goes up into her as if
She now were tree.

All wild moan speaks a series of playful
Chance seeming sounds the happening air
Rolled to a drama of minutiae
played by arbitrary strings or branchings.

Up
into lofty canopy the mind
And all time that was.
She
tenders thought    brings to her
Knowledge of leaves
shoots glistening above familiar
within trance below who issues

Holds beating release our World's Clock

body within body

brain within brain

slowly

birthing

## PLNIPLOI'S PRIZE

Love is not what he's after but what sky's vaulted realm.

*EKSTONISTIAN*  PLNIPLOI slowly speaks
*Is only an extension of the temporal*
*Within Daemonic existence*
*I alone control.*

*Her Being does not exist*
*But has fallen*
*into might I possess*
*Whether by time bringing prophecy*
*Or as it brought AHNÁHR*
*here  all*
*Must land  within flat sphere*
*My throne alone must occupy.*

*Escape from my power is doom.*

*All that exists*
*All essential bearing*
*All that calls  triumphs  all*
*Succor one Being's existence*
*To me belongs  alone to me*

*I am the writing on the wall.*

*Within histories of men*
*their angelic wishes toward nothing*
*Totemic spirit of even wood I am.*

*A single eye the eye of space.*
*A single vision the screen of time.*

*I am the understanding and the way.*

*I am the one prophetic urge now realized.*

*All positions*
*Usurped and marked*
*And by this room*
*Only I    will its entrance.*

*I force compliance*
*Which no other might understand*
*For the common purpose of universal contention*
*This flat throne's circular power*
*Voided of any other apprehension.*

*I am the geometer of light and dark.*

*I      the mask men wear.*

*I am the murderer of the realm of* THERSEYN
*And have cut off beatific sight he might activate*
*Or spell by* EKSTONISTIAN's *flight to safety.*

*Cowardice is what she is.*

*I will*
*To travel toward* AHNÁHR'S
*Toward the Daughter's*
                *precessional axis*
*A fallen world to redound*
*To* PLNIPLOI.

*I have done away with bombardment to and from* OKEANOS.

*I have existence eternal wrapped within me*
*Signaling to the ends of time and space*
*The final solution.*

*I am the new God.*
*Being*
  *drains its elixir into my "poetic."*

*I have consumed ages of difference*
*The puny stars into matter*
*Within slow wind-down of time and space*
*Where work alone will become freedom's goal.*

*I am*
  *the destroyer of worlds within worlds.*

*I am*
  *the new calculus.*

## ONÖNYXA's BED

THERSEYN comes

sight now filled

Time resonating within cellular worldliness
Pulls down beauty
Pulling off the actual

ONÖNYXA

Whose flirtation with time he sees
In a rush of white
A rush of glistening limbs.

Why was this separation permitted
That he would have to play at winning
For his own
    beats in compliance not his own
In the ground of an entire planet..... . .

It cannot be the mere angle of error
But bodies have a precedence
And spell over their souls
Activating desire within the World-Eggs
Fires    sparks a music of relief
That death itself seems a long-forgotten vision.

They fall back in humus
the wide bed
Smoking the worldly cigarette
Sending plumes over the edge of Earth.

Nothing would have kept the com-position from themselves.

Were these two but guises of the real?

THERSEYN'S seed

roots in shade

Of EKSTONISTIAN's copse
And all he brought was but a moment
Held for eternal contention never ended.
There was no cause and effect
And the world goes on as ever.
A subjective train for every existence
Found her breath
To anneal the world's objective essence….. . .

They walk the naked floor
Ghosts or eidolons of a culture long extinct.

This pregnancy
Has more sustenance than the vain glitter of all thought.
They carnally wooed all mankind
And set all relation within their Being
Bearing it.

They might even be taken for a new genus and species
Enfolding within each other's lips
To sleep each's Being beyond the other's.

Was this error the history of mankind?
Do bodies dream in the Earth?
Are they light as air over us
Composing but a solo flight toward the Other?

The cellular's stationed within their entire desire
Driving one another as if to *mean* the other
As if to pass beyond even death.

Entitlement of an end.

Did OÖND stir *me*?  Or OOM?
Did *I* seek OOM in the depths of myself alone?

Was *I* possessive of THERSEYN
EKSTONISTIAN  AHNÁHR

just as Earth obsesses in a chemical mass

precessing neither equation nor formula?

# Norse & Forra

… *fjorsegi frann* … : … GLEAMING (fulfilling) life-muscle …
*Fáfnismál*, 32

O flight,
bring her swiftly to our song.
She is great,
we measure her by the pine trees.
H.D.

first sketch]

bird-song early the cold morning eye saw black torn cloth in the bare branches connecting to thrown expectation awareness a world emptied instanting power power from any ground heard barely seen below was *again* is? what *is* *what* is

*was*?

*was* ONÖNYXA our idyll out of the paleo into the meso-near this gain of soul reverberating hunter's kill loss of soul animal implacement she knew to be alien shape not *his*

thus consciousness born upon the leaving exiting run-away from the walls replay of Troy replay of any and all history destined from out of palladin shape early enzymes or smaller empires even the protean imaginal conquest the images encapsulate vacated then vacating ONÖNYXA beginning idyll the figure and also investment of first person to view this consciousness stripped away her sense of loss birth *is* true replacement of any former implacement orients all our intention

she knew and knows still in not knowing whereabouts of her form the other merely an animalian stasis stuck potential transcendence mating in the world's images

so sings or sung the vowels of unending love all human time still seeds encodes and harbors release and articulating breath a god or virtue a protean form breath daemonic in the cold morning eye torn cloth from barely sexualized limbs the arbor

to the roots the making of tree as conscious desire

consciousness lovely desire married each other in the human hint and glint imagination gone on beyond it even

replacement growth eternal ejaculation human form potentially realized

no doubt empire still to learn every lesson the corpuscled breathing semblance of man this cold morning

*is*

follow-up sketch]

shakes loose his sighted prey for wilder hair

accept the torn then the caught
ONÖNYXA taught teaches reaches these sketches from the paleo-far into the meso-near in our hearing
unabled by holistic as autistic fate QAPTAKUSS
brought himself in the form he'd killed
her voice she sensed loss moan travel
into land again vacant indigenous specter (meso)
realized as *moment* drew her feet into plains and the table-top world flattened Earth by endless search no round world to bring us into this work or view yet
grew in form of search unknowingly
desire knows replacement of the false animal he killed
she to take her life into dead interpretation
thus OÖND and OOM grew carnal *legacy* from every shape she then came to sleeping form enveloped by it as sleep dreams sacrificed soul-host
OÖND
realization of her own kind form *and* desire
consciously lovingly
signal begins imagine
"I"

fourth founding of past and present of sketches
time to show difference for all time]

of night and day
desire again desires and the forms of it
still teased by extinction
holds one to another differentiated to one another body holds daemonicly this loss and gain as imaginal source to material organizations categories become *the* figure human kind can conjure out of absolutely nothing life and death are not nothing

ABRCLÉA
came from this instant and still comes to this instant at the mention the moment love's species bicameral arboreal as the night oceanic seeking as the day in turbulent waves seeks define or know a shore's true length
sees coiled to its shell the soft seeking foot upon the limb of a mossy tree bark or shell too the snail

or also further conjured undulant sea-water's calcinated coral bone
caught under skin plays at catching within itself in secret secure safe to discover under
aspirant in either the lost past
diastolic day
or
emanates imagined joinings by pressure of light in darkness

## SKULD : FIRST-THROWN RUNES

Three Giantesses
        at the well waters the root of Yggdrasil
Runes upon the World-Tree
        scanning   spanning named spans
Tolling in miniature fate
        future stature its gait's skeleton its flesh

                    lips
          eye-lashes
                creak open:

          *tools of HAR-height*

        *VÆTTIRI of waste*

          *dredged testical clouds evaporating*

                *dry forgetful*

        *re-members ÒTHIN's own offspring*

                    *must find speech to fill us.....*

## sketches ABRCLÉA]

ABRCLÉA marks both day and night turning them away from the possible eternal or infinite potential legacy of OÖND and OOM and as the second the other part the newly arriving infinite seed the heart of humankind horizon vibrates
ONÖNYXA ABRCLÉA
turns and wheels infinite caught catch the species left to right substance and insubstance merging their historical moment by these two
once again I play at re-definition daemonicly urging asymptotic realization archaic the ancient the far far paleo running right up to the most near elemental intimation of my body's living touch to rise or fall within this moment
rounding flatness of ancient and before after and contemporary penetration each to the other breaks me into completion extension by virtue of EKSTONISTIAN ONÖNYXA's created cousin I inhabit once again joy-centered insurgence

before these emanations refounded the entire construal of our species ONÖNYXA in the morning by the river led out of the mountain the dream the one night the sketches strewn about the table-top our mind gone into her figuration

ONÖNYXA
pausing in the water round her ankles feet now cold by touch of this living stream mountain stands as night as distance she's uncovered dream preceding this world over here like water the words come evolutionarily do thus echo her stance in the trees on softer grit the riparian gazes toward running thaw-rush downward whitewater braiding rapids leaping into spray and surge dew-like on her back as she descends the highland features spruce twigs burgeoning needles sap odor in her nostrils her half-open mouth
birds met in a plashing chorus water near her path herons and Hábrók hawks riding the crease's flow bathing ravens crossing now one then two

aloft to sit in the pine's lean branches
one more sheltering tree a place to rest she beneath ravens follow but a gleam also to the air the arboreal landscape becomes pronounced her breathing quickens broken branch crackling sound sends a group of ducks up the river's shore *meiðr* she articulates and again *meiðr!* lips vibrate the word wettened echoic up it sounds the trunk the young white pine-pole-trunk

principle reflection the top of her concern now tending daylight catching a band of blue thru many birches differing green spruces cedars redwoods long rows of standing pine

lower ground moving into attention given by travel to catalog air above the path images flicker out of retinalia sparks mirrors red pine needles the highland floor ambling down recording skin feeling taking notation the change in the slope the movement thru this world translations of her time in the slope

leaning into the tread she comes to her dream truncation

stars erupting over this sloped ravine green-black subdued breath against a forra pine sleeps piled little yellow and brown fallen needles and seeds

eyes in the past now? *OOM could have had these* ONÖNYXA dreaming she is lifting hands off OÖND placing them on the eyes of OOM a thousand owls shift in the tree-hole above her head *OOM is dead!* in her dream ONÖNYXA is dreaming of eyes in the night ghost or animal shape to the eyes of OOM ONÖNYXA grieving in her panting sleep by the pine needles the seeds rips out of dream-sleep for the imprisoned image of OOM image liberated from its history

in the night stars begin to slip curving aurora her dream's creativity whole constellations fall to the ground

claiming daylight woke into her born state body made no demand becomes itself up out of loss

animal soul blackened the autonomous she remembers image in the world once again given to the histories of other species ours yet to be made ONÖNYXA knows now OÖND and OOM were an entrance into gods only

each descent from one another unnoticed and no one to know themselves undescending belief she takes note by the feeling skin under the growing verdure growing wooded lee-side dip the valley ravine the braided waters leading touches presence as the scene the same in her and it god-like implacement the figure of them too images in the daylight play with images from the night thrown and being thrown by the collective descent of her and them before the difference of night and day arrive in the future up ahead procreative inspiration generations of generating fallen nightimes upon the world she moves

spreads before her for which she descends

way

leads

down

encountering pines vertical fall to any climb might return such a falling both directions felt in the feeling the yearning the balancing act

a stand of short ash and elm

pines flourish burning nostrils mouth and eyes to the bark she leans and sticks sleeps another night hard resin forms an amber glob hair on a pillow of pine-cones unnoticed

hardens a cone twig together holds her hair in place one with this place in the shape of stiffened resin adheres to her hair

clearing at the level of a ridge round it turns dizzying divide sky-fallen land far as the eye can see itself within notices leaning curving pine forra pine an arch and bend to its main body giving into a new branch leaf twig green ever middle-aged long needles approaching grasps then rubbing between her palms vigorously needles scatter where they might needles commenting on her own name each needle with resin carries over into the air all about her

pattern of movements down into the world their branches which hold the meaning of the tree as night approaches once again the meaning of the tree in shadow still the forra seeming to close in from behind the night takes all the tree into itself and night is it it is night's dilution toward dream dream enters the living proof of experience the fluid interbodily touch seems to be the tree itself symbol interpretation of this time in motion and change power in resin resonates unfolds long before we came to her sleeping beneath the forra tree this sketch was a theoretical anomaly now part of the streaming sap the tree's dream our species had has access carried into not the light changing merely resin a drug or soporific in form of a tree changes in the changeling nature of change changing stills in the deepening movement of articulating day toward enveloping night time no longer she relates the carriage of tree the night the meaning all one into another meta-way all entrance trances accumulate

approaching dream she sees past root might form her previous to this change change itself as code magic channel out of the ordinary out of the pronounced day

who

writes these mornings? who

stays behind traveling

into Earth's deep bowels

ONÖNYXA

her name a bird call

or sight when time of day returns only for her now generation change owns all is her's

down toward ravine the hollow of this extant world maybe reflected image the past dream might show its value

alone the value

tall stands of pine large groves gathering on the ridges needle floors echoing floor needles matted in crunch to heighten senses of memory feeling from back or when in time of change

back it was or maybe night won't come ever maybe she comes within it only alone signal moment pause presence behind stills the echoing floor in a mirroring

moon blanched between pursuit from passing past whose night now stalls its white ONÖNYXA turns toward pines in twilight closing upon itself figure tall inter-graceful specter the tree she'd seen long leaning arching pine walks or attempts to walk into the shadow to the piney floor graceful in the way of escape from the bright moon effect shadow seems half-magnified limbs just now come to life

you?

across the moon above the curved pine boughs    contradictory moment when light and not-light meet    multitudes gather    this MANI    his appearance as god paused between two movements forward back    gloam eyes harbor the past the future    reflection incarnate god ONÖNYXA did not re-seek mingles within the still night air    MANI's wave upon the white screen slight distant echo sucking torch lamps constellations behind this season    contour shed from dailiness awkward stance trudge gives way upon needled floor feet approaching out of the reflection's shadow

screen white screen memorialization she's encountered synthesized    synths now in final exhalation animal shapes across the canvas moon MANI draws    little god or plateau the moon's full time ideal human by all white light reflects light    she settles beneath the pine    seeing *was* believing    forgetting the tall figure who walked this very spot into umbra into lightless life light yearns to integrate and overcome in the brief reflecting moment edge of shadow    singularity

## Verdandi : second giantess

spreads her jaws wide over half-human gaits
Tits
flopping heaving chest-rasp
Old age synthesizing lost past lives
syllabic
chambers of the World-Well:
rimes
root-giant Earth
rime
frosty night-breath
HVERGELMIR spring
cold water and boiling sources
race of ÉLIVÁGAR and GINNUNGAGAP
A proceating movement from Yggdrasil's root
NIFLHEIM heard creak voices images
godless beings from a story's lonely guts

ephemeral icy eras
entrancing the warmth which burns in
rune-melt toward re-implacement:

*Chattel freed*
*universal honor*
*arrested*
*groaning bodies grinding Mammon*
*up thru hardened cracks from the old war*

so that at morning again she feels elbow joints encircling
tired midriff bore the riches of an intensified arboreal night
shoulders a plate for the glaucous head

ABRCLÉA

syncategorial food eaten ONÖNYXA    into and out of all things
pertaining her past her presence swelling unifications of limb and ambulation
*is* flight
tenderly gray-green hair kinked about O's cheeks    long fingers on O's belly    leg muscle
sweat sap mingle    closely napping resins oozing
so the past had come to pass as ONÖNYXA began to wake    allegory the
presence of MANI's screen    figures clinging to one another for interpretation in the materi-
al realms    moon-screen his overlook he the overseer the arch seer the son of Mundilphorra
(*sic*)    melds morning star into calendar    by the boughed the arching pine    seeding new
encounter once was told    written    shown

ABRCLÉA

joins thru longing bodies of tree and pine and her new human form is a
longing    overlapping ONÖNYXA in the invisible phanic consideration of touch
deserted or even mountainous moment    each eye which now cannot be traced    eras-
es    coming to life here ABRCLÉA    the writing and the poem a love-making threading
of seed-cone and hair resinous a-gleam in the translation of the possibility of overlap    no
longer allegory or story    mountainous scenery left vacant in low clouds
æry joining day and night

## EARTH : GIANTESS AT THE WELL

URD
unfolds her long limb
tap-dancing round the Well
tossing every rune into one pile:

*One two one and two two and one*
*One and two two and yolk*
*Timefell cock-crow sky-cock to come*
*Gallus Galdr sings in the ditches all undone*

*Perched on the high tree*
*Come to the end-fight*
*Rips our world from*
*Stem to stern from*

*Branch-crown to root-ball*
*Everything'll burn everything'll freeze*
*Gold is what comes of him*
*Gold the goddess and the gap*
*Beginning to end and*
*Ending beginning him all over again*

sketches ABRCLÉA]

ONÖNYXA opens her mouth sitting up up again to ask certainly to be certain her strange gift in the form of lithe

*Why me?*

ABRCLÉA

flat needled fingers now her own bending knees on the rock turns her face the rich blue just above the slope ridge becoming misty lightly filled lightly clouded grey eyes piercing the distance eglet or Hábrók hawk with its hawklet

*I miss the Yew stood there to my own*

*I was the forra there they took the fire did*

ONÖNYXA

for the first time recognizes pine of her new friend's origin where Yew might have been

*It's burnt over time and time*

*I came out of the fire myself you know or do you?*

*But you're green!* ONÖNYXA shrieks then giggles

ABRCLÉA grinning immensely

*Maybe not a Yew but she was so lovely tho But I saw you coming down from the shadows To show you the Yew* says ABRCLÉA *I knew it was possible* walking down to the crest the ridge behind the pines needles crunching tenderly O. is following ABRCLÉA's gait swaying long stride now a graceful stride moving downhill not as awkward but still the trace of tree up a little awkward but holding still to her movement wind whispers they come to the Yew's stand

A. at the place where the tree would be *let me show you this tree* and out of nothing fog maybe lifting burned off by the day *one of the only here* she says A. says *as you can feel and also see by this circling veins how they circle?* A. puts the branch in O.'s hands

whorls of black mold spinning scars seared darkwood lightwood trance of liquid stillness

*Yew this is the northern most* and as she speaks the tree disappears into the pine-stand behind the all-around

ABRCLÉA comes and moves forward path now they launch descends to dizzier following sky-lines out of many pines ABRCLÉA stops turns ONÖNYXA's eyes flash to attention *let me show you*

ONÖNYXA's eyes wide

*let me show the hornbeam see the nestled branches a low cousin of mine see?* ONÖNYXA approaches the low tree searching for trunk sticking her head into the hanging leaves branches the bush-like tree a kind of social greeting maybe a first of its kind in the evolution of trees and O's kind homo sapientia ?? speaks within

*oh!* she exclaims under curtain of the hornbeam *oh!*

now with her head out from under excited she's found in her palm prickly fruit

*hazels twinned hazels*

*crack 'em open* A. says *go ahead*

under the prickly spiney covering shiny nuts a kidney shape white meat *go ahead* O. eats nibbling the green flavor the savor chewy good green sense running thru bringing saliva to mouth lips with bits of chewed nut-meat smiling O. is without any memory for the first time from beginning now it begins without her moment a test perhaps evolution of her form or pure-minded sense her true kind coming forward

near-land developed and is the taste of any history or memory another life or even another faint intuition birthing or giving birth tending to the far

might read this place she sees the center of seeing as the eye might see itself in its sense as preternatural naming agency of all agencies

this sense ONÖNYXA has now with ABRCLÉA

illuminates in green-grey flame out of all writings as imagination interpreting for itself and in itself

black pine O. brought to make way down ridges slopes with water far below in and out of shade the day wore on and days

black pine slate-like bark layered pulled off by A. handed to O.

sun full on the round large trunk lived age off the edge the mountainous slope caught ridge and the ledge's lip

huangshan pine in the mist in higher sights how many worlds of pine both near and far ABRCLÉA pointing to its thrust into open air now proving by this point pine can reveal and also be hidden new human intelligence both pine-like and thought-like

at the overhang slope forces them abandon path across toward steps of another plateau

sighing struggling two just below the chinese pine the huangshan pine as a kind of world-tree neither indigenous nor foreign but a family which consumes all the clades all the names in itself as it is growing for itself

O. and A. drop another altitude resin holding dust seeds to their skin and skin

suddenly tears water from ABRCLÉA's eyes the tiny relative the very young *Marianas* the purple cones the short green spruce needles    up in the jammed corner of rock    memory she'd share with ONÖNYXA    as if hushing out the world below and above in the human A. brings primal wonder to O.

whispering leaning to her ear    whispering    memories coming fast    far in the past before transformations in the phanic    *don't despair never doubt as long as others in here see look can you hear me?*

O.    silently nodding    raised by this commingling secret shared raised to the level of the heart a formerly wooden embrace our species the intimates I thought I knew defining them this freedom maintains without fantasy stalling it

proof of known and unknown both    phantastical work all dream finally put to work

blue pine fascicles droop and A. is holding her glaucous fingers to compare them for O.'s eyes wide now giggling actually squinting in the comparison

now a tree the tree she is also was    ONÖNYXA's eyes then glass a cone between blue pine fascicles the stiff new friend the beautiful ABRCLÉA    crystal cone visible eye-flash and fingery pine blue pine needles in the gaze of glass with hints of hues

fluid was and is companionship now to the amber resin of the pine's trunk    pine's veins    telling future sap    where they all go these two are channelling    sea calling within both    vein's calling them too    sea's sound all fluid's relations

now all movements two can tell    they do not love one another out of nothing exclusively    changling nature did implace one to the other    pine held still holds motion because it is the metamorphed ABRCLÉA    holding the work    gripping clay on the slope    downward to the sea they both can hear in their joint

two who    come    not of the magic of wish    enveloped by spell    MANI's moon-screen embraces in material heavens inter-speciated thru their moon-birth

red pine brought them back the encircling world geographic terrain they will tell
much as O. brought in destiny she charges meso-near with animation out of old Norse too bringing all endings into place near the pine    out of Mundilphorra as the father image MANI the god image of the moon-screen    bringing each fyrr in mid-oestrus ignites wafting fragrance beginning world-embalming activations of RAGNARÖK

they are biological memorialized agencies    chords no longer wandering    will be    circumference of her fyrr's incense    sap burnt one time and only once neither as daughter nor mother

*acchordeont*

O.

*by the cock's cry*

*involuntary concordance of volition*

*runes also hold in skalding by each tree*

*alphabet or language future hosts*

*in its language when it sings it*

scots pine the japanese red pine orange-red bark in the genus pinus in the phylum world
A. shows different kinds of wood soft white wood yellow or hard wood

western white pine beginning also ending is in one world no inner no outer    eastern white pine longevity extends the tower time seems to build so shows possibility of eternal peace : *hereafter*

*theophanic*

*MANI's moon-screen*

*gleams from itself by virtue of this tree which is now aligned with these two as neither lineage nor the legacy of any estate but what after-world arrives*

Yew grows out of this slope male here the other cones pollinate one another
A. reaches as O. grips and strips the comb of needles into her fist opening palm both sniff the pungence
here in alter egoic trip O. and A. collaborate
exemplification prophetic time descends
mountain air now a fountain from rocks at the cliff's edge trail winds to sea they see below coming closer sound rising to meet with them as two examples
we write the bringing which brought the living specter of this queering friendship when pines come alive and the mouth waters
foundations of writing are as little fountains little jets announcing milking of each sappy branch resinous dew interpretation penetrating each syllable rhyming tones upwardly moving tune our O. source in study to ABRCLÉA seeks her wooden ear teach us touch tune every epode falls from source-height caught by the tune ONÖNYXA's moment?

sketches re-zoomed]

ontic library the myopic has many needles on the hand of ABRCLÉA onto-logical library rather it is an archive the ontological the ontic moment ONÖNYXA accessing or has potential to access her own personal reading overcome by nearness ABRCLÉA's animating presence pointing pushing pressing her gaze in this magic meeting behind it all she also sees time interprets momentary feeling encounters images retinal interpretating potencies witness ABRCLÉA's and this travel thru time the touch which is most moving for the human nothing within time is of any worth but the being of that touch coming or leaving the book allegory or standing in for this or that touch de-parts the form of the Book

## GLEAMING : RUNIC THROW FROM THE SKALD'S EYE

Urd runs nine runes into the branches of Yggdrasil
        10,000 legs and feet in suspended animation
    turns to her others in the poet's eye
            (now wholly joined thru skies):

*MIÐGARÐ dwells the human*
    *ASGARÐ descending*
        *legions for VANAHEIM*

*JÖTUNN out of YMIR dwell*
    *ship will bound upon*
        *forthcoming animation*
            *rumored ÁLFAR*

*SKÍÐBLAÐNIR?*

*Sails thru HEL's root*
                *Earth upended.*

*COMPANIES OF STONE seem not to move and*
    *dwell in dark magic.*

*RIME in NIFLHEIM*
    *sheds the World-Tree's dew-frost at dawn*
*Swallows FENRIR's mouth his teeth gleaming as sense-notes*
    *letters    names and shared life-spells re-continuing.*

Now list and compare nine worlds to the one tree by these skrys.

sketch     rune-notes]

## Recessed roots

deep de-capitation of MIMIR

moment  the mime from the rime

Yggdrasil's distillation

ÒTHIN's bartered eye :

drunkeness    boisterous for release :

to be known now

seed unfold crease wrinkle the bark of man overwhelmed symbolic falling cone figure now positive enlightenment mind ruled against she comes to her own begun in sound as speech in a kosmos errant shot or election of tone attention neither seen nor telling of scene commences its momentum

created interest sympathy mounts a mystical trump

holding marks by memory the body's turf ONÖNYXA holds (*phaïnts*) theo by her body's rhythmic beckoning the man calling his shadow by form's symbiotic force-field

interpreting marks incisions intaglios thus seen

arborglyphs ephemeral names

*Picea abies* to accentuate growing warmer climate our plane trees of the north not all to grow could be imagination to some as seeds too

runic throw might help that reach limb in glabrous feature the seam of world/underworld bald statements

as if these things ABRCLÉA handing to O. seeds time by her entry into vision

recess over and this is the downside to the sea children no longer no speaking of the eye/I small games are over the bigger begins

out of the screen the selenotropos the throw clusters new game cones of the spruce she shows us coming together galloping fusion the rune now plays as sun and rays within a quality of night body's a force-field a source-code running comment

*Picea schrenkiana* hairy half-cones holes in the nut-like extension

*Morinda spruce* *Abies pindrow*

"The shoots are smooth and glabrous (hairless)"

ONÖNYXA wants now to know where we are    mystical pine tree merge to the lotus DVERGAR stone holds imaginary key the underworld they've left in highland    descend into    one another    path the sense given giving slightly opens circles    toward the sea destination rising vertically    in sound    *timbre* all about them    green needles in clusters    green-grey intimations

soaking deodar cedar bark in water at the base of the pine's root    dunking hair she washes O.'s hair    perfuming her    poem's rise

ABRCLÉA now cries begins to weep a kind of naming emanating recognition    pines over the edge of this slope

*How many!    Look!    Each in the same forest!*

silence which all of them in a mass hymning by the wind plays thru    beginning    never separated    into time

so coming to know ABRCLÉA ONÖNYXA now sees within the nature of the beloved both verbal and subject

slope down from her past only in separations of gone time    yearning now toward A. does not recall to O.'s gone time    can't recall repair before or after the rift in gone time

neither owned nor owning devoted to the cry in gone time

recognition

A.'s voice

pines

## sketches ABRCLÉA]

human divisions categories or clades

kingdom: plantae
division: pinophyta
class: pinopsida
order: pinales
family: pinaceae
genus: pinus

here end-rhyme contains our future rhythm where we go off in search of seeds nuts sap

the most interesting aspect of the entire genus pinus whether they be monoecious or dioecious the cones differences for release times different manners pollinated thru different methods stuck are some by resin the whole cone so tight

stiff only fire melts the fragrant sap dispersing contents finally into the common orb

if we are in this genus we have to back into the clade to discover interdependence the proliferation of symbiotic relationships consider the bird a figure of the poem finally wholly distributing genus has no other way to drop to fertile soils reason a way to move the categories limbs see justify animation while in flight

because cones amassed in preference to undistinguished non-revelation prefer to be forever their sealed hardened incubation no name good enough no time ripe enough for their dispersion their poem asserts before after this poem does their world

mass matter the pleroma the very educated catechism of undifferentiated existences the void out of which is taught all issues their catechism's broken open by this poet

into the figures of O. and A.

into naming choirs agencies who have thrilled to one another's company without seduction of the educated classes statisticians of expanding cladistics interpretations of a grand design they themselves long for

who cannot commit to suffer this world one peep alongside the longing not one emittance from the heart's valve sulphured match-tip sets against them into eternal configurations of eschatological diaresticals

as from the first sketch a strike against all surface

beaks against nuts of hardening categories
κατη the source name calls *down*
χεῖν chism's derived *holding*
*has an* ἔχω somewhere in it
an echo
brought to indoctrination
χέω *to sound*
the *achene* now cousin of this root
*aching* encasement

disseminates thru newly naming

ONÖNYXA wakes in the mountain air now tuned to the sound ABRCLÉA has given her as touch so that naming these pines associations here echoing thru woods down the slope

memories of another mountain now rouses she wanders from the needle bed butterflies fluttering to boughs cling and feast on needles

walks in a fascinated echo of feet treading under branches

hears in bird chatter blushing changing the place they were living and where they lay to find and speak eyes wide in excitement to tell

*did you hear the exchange it was an echo an echo locating the most potent seed cones! little armies of watchers watch and descend*! she rapidly speaks

to the ground where ABRCLÉA

*watching us all the time ABRCLÉA watching all the time!*

was

*did you hear them?!*

ABRCLÉA

now a bank of red needles

*ABRCLÉA! Where'd you go?*

is

*ABRCLÉA!*

ONÖNYXA calling thru the sloping pine

then to the path they were descending

*ABRCLÉA!*

ONÖNYXA halts on the inclination hesitates to the past upward on the mountain thinks

*did she return?*

*that way was her home?*

calling

*ABRCLÉA!* *ABRCLÉA!*

## sketch 12]

and too musical phrase from this mouth mouths back the little uvula abyss to the glottis I thought if there were moments here falling off any track vocal consonants as well as aspirant these two for articulation
versions of silence one conjuring ideal the other full blasted real
depths to the *fjorsegi frann* chords folds of the membrane which

(the bird) `Igþan kvaþ :`

| | |
|---|---|
| `spakr þøtti mēr` | `spillir bauga` |
| learned thinks I | this destroyer of ring |
| `ef fjǫrsega` | `frānan æti` |
| if that lifetongue | gleams when chewed |

# sketch 13]

a winding path down to the sea from where you thought you were belief most of all your most high form reflections white in the overlook ridge ONÖNYXA panics but this is the lifeblood of not only our own witnessing but her entire lifetime ABRCLÉA entwined within for safety seeks thru loss
running to near sound down coiling sound the shore oh ONÖNYXA you need wings what wings where moonlight reflection ABRCLÉA once upon a time

takes the form running swiftness beating limbs ABRCLÉA's cousins seeking to find thru them
sight muscled passive to resilient runner muscled brave body adapting
so our species contains

form forms transcendence protean as the greater *hexeity* change itself reaching given needs of us innate

she becomes war-like embodiment desires projected toward the masculine again upheld pursuit their armor heart elemental intimizing ONÖNYXA special entreaty of muscle gleaming in the forms which will be in twilight no matter
his true flight's agency readied by longing inhabits running swiftly within disappearance ABRCLÉA
renews to this seaside wide body from a wave she rides returning

sketch 14 ] something here about turtles who've hatched racing to the surf

loud the meso-near ONÖNYXA's ear he calls her voice to shape re-shaping in the cupped ear shouts out over spumey coils of lips of wave-drop release timed for the music of his heart which calls transposed to finding in the disappearance this coiling threaded spermy world timelessness re-calcinated

story unfolding phenomenal ridges brows of light alone abandonment of light and reflection screen ABRCLÉA walked out of now ONÖNYXA crying knowing the meant-for fulfillment here in each other

collapsing waves flatten into sand imprinting feet he stands transposed

what would rise? surrounds our world a phantastic apparitional imagination the depths the endless finite churning constant likeness to likeness

yet image he sees completely derived from what he now sees?

here O. on the shore below the falling slope is consumed and consuming into bowl oceanic edge O what changes! What singularities!

gods and our god troublesome facings of the depth image incongruous creature on top the water water as if surfing he's an apparition not of substance anymore inherent surf says it as he comes to find and define the shore thru himself as O. is held in question by any possible witness his species in which god's forms find *her* recognition ecstatic wave belongs to *her* before this moment's merge forever now joins *me* to *him* as *she* comes joy ONÖNYXA a two-fold incongruity

unwitnessable but by *us*

streaming from his eyes the water reddened in the deep blue ABRCLÉA rides the cambrous physicalities held her close to treeform of us first animation as if flesh the manifold manifestation of liberation of matters he now sees thru ONÖNYXA

a pivot her body shell or muscled form of him

riding toward us from the oceanic no longer conjured from the moon but from safety of their ever possible and promised concealed abandonment in one another

## sketch 15 combining HUGINN and MUNINN]

ABRCLÉA cipher now on the wave come to shore and to the imprinted neo-knowledge returned to the source of her animation the elemental pre-dawn temporal insignificance waves and limbs and wind night and sound and stars will not kill her self to spite his new nor blame change whenever wherever

multitude of shells on her skin had once been treeborn bulk and bark flesh of her rebirth oceanic descent washes up on shore where ONÖNYXA stands

crying elation at many recognitions

ABRCLÉA his loved guide now vertical replacing horizontal nature of OÖND and OOM

again the appearance dear reader out of what has disappeared her species will finally know his

ABRCLÉA tumbles into sand shells the hollowed pink blue feet attach to white half-conch before ONÖNYXA drops onto the reappearance in foam embracing apparition muscle ABRCLÉA not so much to hold *her* once again nor to examine *he* becomes wakes shifting

ONÖNYXA form wrapping arrival kissing

themselves embracing signal energies sleeping in the out-of-nothing patterns of this same coupling shore's clouds north south flame burns senses all sensuals ever a-knew

changing interpretations presence always to one another as the grand together all are practicing place of articulation identities enable view judgment of content by length and alignment they hold and make by each other

friendship into elevated realms sand and loved and beloved *each* a shadow form feeding one another imprinting yearning by any withdrawing each to their face to see both far and near afraid of one another then too visits all interpenetration

and from this into night becomes them

light their peaceful triad coiled about the other beloved form in shadow's suggestion might have had its way with

each another reaches thru to grooves houses them all in starshape while the night comes on

ONÖNYXA sighing in the hold of ABRCLÉA's home shell-encasement round the hole circular spy-ring of celestiality's return primordial embrace of night stars in transit and entrance his entrancing ONÖNYXA's traveling eye into ABRCLÉA's view into his holding telescoping view pinioned upon sidereal review anew here

crustaceous anemones

flying jellyfish

star-crossed star-fish coral exposed by night-tide luminescent water sparks nervous constellations energies illuminating this cave in the clouds

cave and nacreous secrets all others before and after confirming their intentions below in echoic proteins and calciums lipids and homes holding initiation of him they perform too by her shore-return shushing this nightworld to bed

establishing ties and loose arrangements light and matter beloved awareness tattling elbowed oxter night's odor informing nostril claims crab's carapace houses breath's intake catenated lights thread their outlines electrically morphic states projects them as desire but thru-out the kosmos they were a psychic species heart-valves spitting salt alchemical distillations of their many arrivals into one another

into substance their secret view dense reef-light the liquid black world

## RAGNARÖK sketches

the already heard or known    infrapsychismic    jointure of stratocumuli]

= MÚSPELL moving into showdown of crepuscular light and crystalline ice
cramped horizon  (and as *musulmán* was an adaptation from the arabic divergence for the
term *muslim*    evinces our O. likewise using *his* muscles back into evolution to correct it
reverses the spell)
thaws NIFLHEL at the BILRÖST crevasse by the muscle's new mass
vertical interpolation commences matter
bridge   united all crossing all carrying all interpretation
questions lose significance and the game in contention of fire and ice
south and north    no *one*
figures alone anymore

## appearances]

now in the clouds    gray matter    mist rain pouring the last of its pillars    night
beloved knowings    knew    wears light    winning by cries
languages beginning by loss
worshipped phases    phrasings billowed    architected tincture   sky-witnessing
swallowing blackness feints toward midnight
threatening rumor's triumph

## semblances]

hidden designs all design    shadows circulate synaptic nimbus    sidereal opacity
was *pneuma*
now coming thru the end
trick held MOIRA entranced    forever    moves now    sketch's edge commencing
thru the reader
gigantic hubris    reeking
hooded ÒTHIN        misfit outcast wanderer anyone to meet here
*any* one    transfigures the BILRÖST bridge
she gave into him to see loss

sketches ABRCLÉA]

streaming thru two ears    recitals    skaldings
eustachian tube fills with requisite pressure    spiraling cochlea    song asserts itself along a series
evolution    ONÖNYXA receptive stars the manifestations of ABRCLÉA    while I write in supplication    tone tunes one to another without end but the one was    without satiety one
offering neither an end nor beginning    streams the milky substance appraising light calls the hidden quality night is    infrapsychismic inalienation
ears home to the once printed foot    measures    thru-out historical dynamic of written song    notes    odes    scribbled and scratched    descried    setting *voices* in arranged recitation    *voice* rearranging recital

and this multi rhythmic experience trance entirely upwelling expression shapes the beloved    aims our face

upper celestial capital

X

GYFU gift of the 7th rune
GEFION in it too
sun crossing celestial equator    imaginary girdle galactic coil    vernal equinox    northern GEFION whose phonemes change in praise of the southern slope the curve so crosses original diarestical moment ONÖNYXA knew all *her* names *his* one name-change at first ceremony was
sunrise sundown together meeting all portents    see-singing stars seizing scars for the missed era of the body the land the marks of hills and lakes    a catalog of her names now issued by his body

ᛏ ᛞ ᚢ

ᚠ ᛚ ᛃ

ᛉ ᛊ ᚷ

# SEVLESMEHT
## & THE BIRDS

Deluded natures cannot recognize
The royal way that stands before their eyes.
Farīd ud-Dīn ʿAṭṭār, *The Conference of the Birds*

## Ductus Updraft

Great dark parsimony catenating
compounded wings a watery squeal-
Ing expenditure releases up-drafting fat fanning
Blades flapping the billowing residue flocks
smoke smotes the desert sky

Blotted landscape Murmurrating hybrids
specie uncashed
Pre-existent spreads beginning sight
Blinds always the eye's flight
Values without sight
Human History the ocular activity plotted in memorial register

squalling conference accumulates
Resource hears abundant captivated wealth
Serenely raging waves sway tonal vibration
algorithms from available aetherial dusk

Fire off this Earth heat mirage atmosphere fuels
cacophonous beaks
Crowd-sourcing changes
Rise massing immanent
Clear dimension an apparent upper heaven

spatial montage lands in air one moment
losing assumed ground philogenetically owned

Congregations blots conferencing
Concentrated delivery of signal to undo the masses
Under oceanic emissarial emissions bellows
High-pitched semblance sight captured first so long ago

eternal fund      sputtering flame's one flare
universe's conceived knowing acknowledgment

Gestational      correspondent chemical      dirt or ash

whorling up constellate's curious flue

bones
sweat
blood
skin

essence indissoluble future writes burningly now
Prophetic sources gaze upon
Spheric appointments      sun in every world possible
Plains give away from distance
planes and objectives
giving away secret codes
Orbed molecular recapitulation dissolves retrospectively

light's movement wound profound night's creosote to cave-wall

# Transposed World-Tree : "Charm of Impossibilities"

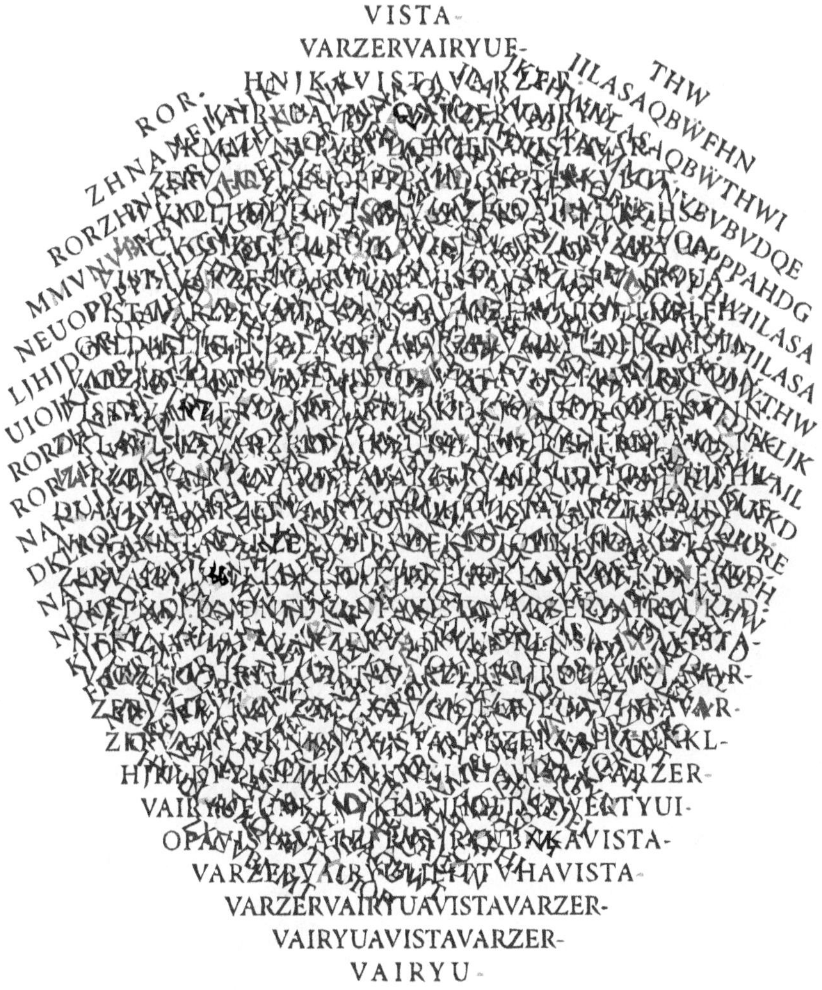

first sketch]

SEVLESMEHT enters shaman's tent-cave to light the fire    finding flame never gone out    of course    fuels    the very matter of all dead things one day visits this special flame only in history we've written so far    heat    more essence lights unseen torch bears each scene    up the middle    newest exile    gesture's furthest human realization

THERSEYN envisions    out of all has caused him or did not cause to be here

he    must attach to other fuel    scraps otherwise keep him an outrider    his attempt at interpretation lost    gathered into meditation

rumor of his own body ritual about to come upon presence never before quite this shadow

focused by exile

knowing body's resource    hand now up

skull

out of migration eclipsing scattering

RED CIVILIZATIONS    threads

nothing but several Gods of drama    war    conflict

crackling burning

## Seen / Un Seen

The end came to civilized embodiments
    receptors enshrined enslaved    pawn or God nowhere seen

At last    total flailing incapacity insubordinate
    Earth
    insubordinate celestial fire underneath PLNIPLOI's coup
    true image    finally human
    withdrew
    inverts summation    twilight feature bodily renders eternity
    infinite unknown transmission

PLNIPLOI    navel out of which the angel of human resource
    passes into rendition of all false or cozzened historicals
    at one with the un-warring specter of himself
    trumps without struggle image without matter
    figuration of limited vocabularies unable to access
    fuel    cold and isolated as death's own
    weather    cemetery cemented
    un-ease ever rises to overcome

These    written circulations    recall THERSEYN
    so that minor characters continue the human door unseen

PLINIPLOI
    gathered into grip    sees as he seizes
    eternity as that can only be taught
Passing inheritance what uninstructed coinides
    as symbolic captivity
    knowledge
    used up and bigger for being invisible like fire

AVISTAVARZERVAIRYU born from this still point
oracular glistening drop celestial pin-prick tone

SHIRU heard fall to planetary hearing

informs timing to historical fictions

S H E wed to hypostatical end of PLNIPLOI

uprisen insurrects self to be her challenge now SEVLESMEHT intimates
ignorant to the infinite garment
spun from star RORZHNAN
inception of all ages

THERSEYN
related her appearance
so that minor to major
which music PLNIPLOI's age might emerge meaningful

AVISTAVARZERVAIRYU
manifests stages

upon sky SĚVLESMEHT be-holds
His wonder heretofore unattributable
role-playing vanished and assumed
sight sees him beginning synonymous
to fire
out of endless sizzling burnt-up limits

second sketch]

of our understanding the crossing ribbon of space the circular nature of what we once named time engaging movements moments land itself re-formed before it entered eternality the light of fire was/is mixing smoke light brought the aspect of PLNIPLOI a capture of revelation light has in fire captured smoke circling doubt abyss not apprehended light not to be released

true as long as SEVLESMEHT can remember but he has no memory anymore no people no job or practice empire of ZAS and MOIRA undone by their child PLNIPLOI as well as other disintegrations over-use under-utilization

a premise subduing actual Earth as other planets will be sub-servient creatures life-forms clinging to each and every planet subdued basest most elemental appearance has not yet been seen the greater struggle

Self comes under presumption but also to valuations of continual burning flame contains light

the entire body humans

direct transmission

toward the eye

captures written memorized turned over and over formed heavens up above believe it or not this errant philosopher SEVLESMEHT changed by way shaman changing roles Sophia's echoic parameter at the edge of his sight

he all at once smoke fire light dependent on transposition of the mythic one fact of the Other

his position nature easily thought belonging to person also angelic discovery in depths of what alchemical foundations the Zoroastrian Magi of the Hellenes "Other" as meaning

confluence of Pythagorean nature-lovers out of storied time came to be known Zoroaster *Zaratos* the mis-interpreter the Greek name the prophet or deity the access point to godhead time fire and light once again Pythagoreans' incessant probing of nature cosmos perpetrates from east to west the figure of the Chaldean (Babylonian) Magus and introduces mythic origins into the Greek world-view

**all told it is sourced to the Avesta language textually introducing *Zervan* shows growth migration a bifurcated meaning the high priest a sort of fallen prophet laws strictly esoteric hence Orpheus holds Zervan his source in the embodiment of verse song sung re-projection elemental originary manifestation burns mortality toward a higher heaven redeemer**

cosmicity penetrates legal identifications we here consider as our own origins translated by Orphic mouth στόμα

individual truly emits existence given to meditation upon this one-time allegory of time (speech)

by which to understand leap as THERSEYN had into sublime all-encompassing void holds destiny holds light

(but these were teachings watered down into absence of religion itself the uprising of the age of ZAS MOIRA the rumors of AHNÁHR and SHIRU the intimations of EKSTONISTIAN and THERSEYN

then

dynamic prophecy he living ribbon of codes infra-entangled essence inferred *enfer-red*

gateway land as struggle to overcome "self" en-used by psychic nearness long hidden possessions in the outrider ridden

seeming seaming seams each self recording their crossing roads flames and tongues sees himself finally

overcoming

## XZIDYAZAG

poured out mother fire
beauty known only in image
forested hidden region
Came to embody form's own transcendence
not so much in personation of form
but infinite reach this world only knows
twinned
Pregnancies     light and dark
manifesting angels     times and ages
incestual     progenerative
seen unknown visitations of light
erecting dark paths in this only world out of Self

And this     angel     she
above others the new
intelligence of angels as messenger
chivalrous inside subsequent sufferings
schools of overlapped labials flames from form

inevitably succumbs to laughter     ridicule
the end     the lie the trick
torn from high notions

beauty seen then
absolute abstract
ugly rejected by present states of knowing out of history

Casts an entire species ensures orders     hierarchies
ladders     views     imprisoned prismed realities

out the body
his beauty

angles upward in drafts crossing trails

SEVLESMEHT
begins in waves of flame
pictures of XZIDYAZAG's appealing
drawing strings threads
thru emptied mirror
calling containment frames
out of lines     the frames
curves

But sound     answering rules
she hears he speaks
spunk derived
spokes the driven words     flames
gestate again
enlightening

real imagined bellies

by leap THERSEYN pre-figured our human realm  considering age the time of SEVLESMEHT's exile  *Ahriman* arrived  inside the projection  Ahriman  here as SEVLESMEHT / THERSEYN duality or twin spirit reprise out of the Gathas anti-thesis to the leap  S. must go the route toward discovering his seeking that leap thru peregrinating chiasmatic tongue of flame

XZIDYAZAG's arrival out of fire always has been **in** the shamanic  the "modern" posture S. has as his nature

divines fire for light but can only come to limited retarded cinema of her he has as one stage of desire  meanwhile the garment the celestial goes unheeded

believed to be where it always was in an age still contains that gallop of historical goals and visions  (n.b.: write a prequel to the sketches elucidating *unearthed* Hsian garment)

S. to come to disappointment of her as his own creation tho beautiful she is nowhere near perfection of aeonic AVISTAVARZERVAIRYU

AVISTAVARZERVAIRYU

waiting specter of Ohrmazd  *Ahura Mazda*  the twin of celestial eternal time  dioscuri the Hellenes fashioned withheld and potioned potented Orphic texts funeral rites  but to no avail  history marched toward inevitable xristianization of the West (or whatever else you want to name it)

and that is all history will ever be good for (mouth full of words) as far as these terms are concerned  sealed away for good  surviving pre-historical gaze now looking at twins of light and dark

out of infinite time Zervan first figure destiny precursor to Angelic holding things in light and dark for their messaging

more to our own point the making fashioning technics the garment celestial stole she wears

prophecy mantle round the method of modernism and in all contemporary goals the putting together the unraveling as well this method the method of "prophet" who must fall down in order to sketch continued from the previous]

S. doesn't know this circular prophecy so he's the exo-coital onanism of retarded or pretend vision jumping and moving around the fire its heat ascendance its light the kept coveted image of the beauty of beauties

image now thru cycles of his own history once again jerking him off in cinematic specter of XZIDYAZAG til he begins to yearn for real skin reality body partner goddess left to be only rumor image still retains

sees yearning interpreted as PLNIPLOI imageless unadorned

yearning *becomes* method urges S. once again to see sight
leap into immolation of the void realize intensity the star AVISTAVARZERVAIRYU

takes her position of thwart blocking Ahriman and darkness blots out smoke interpretive cinematics of Ahriman into the true age enwrapped woven satiety the Goddess's celestial parameter

enveloping his whole being in stillness
forever before
explosive penetration of all methodologies girdles invention

## Creation of RORZHNAN's antecedent

> "... it steps back to watch the forms of transcendence fly up like sparks from a fire; it slackens the intentional threads which attach us to the world and thus brings them to our notice; it alone is consciousness of the world because it reveals that world as strange and paradoxical."
> Merleau-Ponty, *Phenomenology of Perception* (1945)

Living the remotest part of theater
Image flickers lighted flame
                    technique of divination
Vocabulary
                sighting constant absorption

Out of flame light one leap crossing
            fondling self-enclosure of empire
*Pneuma* and *Physis*

        **emergence an asterism unrivaled**

RORZHNAN       with       AVISTAVARZERVAIRYU
SEVLESMEHT     robed
      heat-lick salving his dead conscience
                death of his own death
      empirical records for one
                recently ends
                        personifies disuse his

                            disablement
                    by multitudes and masses

Up against smoke-hole projection an entire civilization

Birds amassing
sky hole
part and entirety
sacrificed eternal rays
shoots weft
threading woof-roof

Visions martial array which ended time
Here embodiment subtle shuttle's

future's regained
origination organizing
ecstatic faults vault feeling
reinstituted
his immolation
withinwards

Her meaning
removal of script
spatio-temporal infinity fittedly strange in RORZHNAN's house

Partnering all wearable interpretation now writes

## fourth sketch]

out of eternal-infinite place veiled name creation never ended

THWIILASAQBẄ

the passive tense might be companion to the activated Gerund
however you want structure in the grammar of time or literary allegorical or performative stance surreal a(e)lludes dimension beyond what is "known" symbolically
all have instant partnership of passive active
eyes ears sees hears what each Earth gives out of aeonic voice projectiles missiles of attention intention their procreative fully funded surge passivity forever pressured connection to leap
origin's light first found as fund

## Iblis Re-deemed: Garment of Fire

THWIILASAQBẄ throws Iblis into world

SEVLESMEHT medium of message
recognizing blockage doubt
cinematic self-doubt
overcomes by self-immolation over and over

Entirety of THWIILASAQBẄ
Shows Iblis

cloud recurrence
past plays present
gaming defunding limited time
self needs prove
transcendence **this** world's context acknowledged

THWIILASAQBẄ indeed passage toward transparency
New learnings not teachings of the game
Touching understanding
memory laid on eyes
a
film

By which **all-seeing**

(AVISTAVARZERVAIRYU)

crossroads of the senses]

he begins returns

moment one place exilic he was

visitations the will pursued his station in spite ignorance comes forward the interpreting angel

birth overlap to all connexions
THWIILASAQBẄ
enables passage thru Goddess
AVISTAVARZERVAIRYU
shows in one limited
gaze his first entering this world basalt basins pools of water caught him out of frames
and diadems the vision he fell thru

purports crystalizations at the fire now

blood as water transforming fire age compels him see ori-
gin his own sight mathesis only cinematic centers the desert of rock base
chemical source persisted within passage because of THWIILASAQBẄ

passage he sees is *Iblis* falling the thrown sense of his coming into world not
entirely demonic except his *own* demon
from this entire prophetic
tradition shaman's root directed toward wrong age now passed

being alone his actualization of thought's prophetic
for which thought and not frames
not calculation but relation
extension origin
his agency
THWIILASAQBẄ

## sixth sense *CINEMAGE* (emergence)]

*parousia* Παρουσία presence of dance around fire then
subsequent leap into fire
passage

unfolds now *miraj*
reaching up into connexion

## THWIILASAQBẄ & MURMUR

Multitudes birds
Capable dialogue and counsel
Squalor of ruins smoke flame
Parsing flow ascension
original birth
Cycling
wheeling wings
wheels within wheels
pattern
interpreting heat smoke squalor
murmur of migration
ribboned trail weaving false eternities demonic lying tongues

Connects shoulders
sounding echoic dimensions of RORZHNAN

AVISTAVARZERVAIRYU's relative infinity in open
blaring light without horizon
pages interpreting invisible book
design
migratory ancient
evolutionary
paired to the pairing birds co-notationally

upward the entire sense divine and what centers
SEVLESMEHT

however

the question of individual cannot either be downwardly impressive or upwardly expressing two positions in common magic pneumatic gesture ZAS for so long embodied the world fell into belief of disbelief itself by his two-ness

not an unbodily proposition the individual puts forth gesture one with breath plays suspension of air and aether which was at the formation first Earth first human mutually dependent *Qi* or middle meso-celestial empire earth air is and always was

individual

out of which the entire system of systems inventions have birth in fire as fuel of light and emptiness a brief breath entire worlds en-cycled

inventions of humans as well mineral biological worlds also "conceived" in wheel evolving descent really ascent into air either principle or belief

carried sub specie or currency of image body might hold when visited by light enlightened so toward itself site for breath's spell re-suscitation origin

~~scratch~~]

previous aeon's identifications psychology of a magician's casted spell
cast to be once again spit from pneuma as parousia

reflected theophanic assembly SEVLESMEHT now *holds* not first not last but because
he's cast

out

out of it the only way to understand the gone senses of the present age
time which cannot be retrieved by the past of the past but in the coming past visage
of vision able to render image to this movement of ascension burning and de-
scension of progressive time

fuels earthly angelic movement by thoroughly covering each reveal

## Re-Manticising Image

ZAS the sublimation of all intents and purposes the demon of history lyed into our skins deepening deathless endless speech seeking enfold you me more into the phenomenal world as his phenomenon

MOIRA sublime carrier of that egoic cogitating
So then
PLNIPLOI entered to level life toward himself
prophetic by the phenomenon of self alone

Yet out of like lonely isolation
Desolate casting spell and lungful potion
Recipe un-acknowledging beauty
Played the role of roles until

**f i r e**

refractions of the star RORZHNAN
incestual recognitions process
distance into nearness
numinal disinterestedness
ensnaring any other mantic antic by this one

So fire
ejaculating SEVLESMEHT
Threw his essence to burning conveyors
Fueling witness to light's creation
Whereby dark and night
self-impregnation might
Turn three worlds humanity's thought
toward inevitability
Closer to any pantheon
by luminescent spunk

Out of this waiting prophetic image of engine
Mankind's inventory of invention
Rolling flames from wheels gears foretelling dynamism
          shot
                    into hinge beauty distilled

**THWIILASAQBẄ**

toward doctorate SEVLESMEHT realizes he belongs to tradition foundation hard empiricism vanished empire appearance of witch-doctor and shaman both apparitions docetic attributes of transparent attitudes light out of dark dark out of light last note in one become first note tone in the other prophetic movement various transpositions resemble groupings modes Messiaen and his play with composition alongside open ear-canal toward birdsong captured the *quartet* itself over and over

many limited "impossible" modes yet together or in composition portray openings toward totality whereby flights but actually symphonia of sight found the birthplace of sight each original sighting correspondence with various cosmogonic light-sources order of angels issuing THWIILASAQBẄ

yet assembly made according to correspondence the person of AVISTAVARZERVAIRYU Goddess of absolute time she out of circles spheres nor placed in them by mere operations or functions other than prophetic passage order person attending the pantheon surpasses its number by ingenious passage "charm of the impossible" not extended fallacy of empiricism (that speech) nor simply a turn of phrase by which we know someone is embodiment swallowing all four directions this trimester thinks as it encounters thought by experience we neither forbid nor give to speaking voices without that tongue

## eleventh ]

creation of self-tardiness delay in the progress of the world unconscious revolution begun to pitch the angelic against human history albeit denied by any and all epochs ages the very same cast-away non-purpose contains seed to all future reasonings in the cloaca of the brain-case

somewhat hard to understand while empire in full swing here now
simplicity smoke air fire light wheeling iconostatic existence SEVLESMEHT who has no need for onto-theology education's purpose nor logos but the docetic enterprise of transparency seeing thru all portioning event every substance into one passage THWIILASAQBẄ to attain the presence of AVISTAVARZERVAIRYU

once thought contention even polemic dissolves in her mode
birds a permanence of associative song modes of transposed scales keys and harmonies all within multitude or mass as at one time blockage the sun or light at another time opening toward light measuring echoing light's apparitions within person who tends the smoke-hole as well the fire below stoking creation thru embodiment of image and image's home in flux thru THWIILASAQBẄ comes

future in form of mode of the impossible

## Now finally epiphanatic joining : Quartet for the End of time

"Their melodic contours, those of merles especially, surpass human imagination in fantasy .... volleys and trills of our little prophets of immaterial joy ..."
Messiaen, *La technique de mon langage musical (1944)*

Four birds       cross roads

Blackbird Nightingale Merle and Chat

Out the Abyss Time emerges

Prefigures

Depth the muscular movement

Opacity Anthropoidal

THWIILASAQBẄ
epiphany       banality
opens its Angelic inventory
crosses     crossing light
updraft       changeover       end of the prophet/shaman

shaman wears each invention of light

ultimately diaphanaticly
merges nor suspends mirroring by will
nor empire

its cousin historical (outdated) reason the prophetic hand
thought to master by way of a static presence in the present tensings of time's habits
behavior psyche thinks to hold fast

our world given to ordering symbolic articulation
full

Deserted
music the heart's dark cloister

Assumes end of time all the time

## the last sketch]

between old magician ZAS whose *pneumatic* arc up to *nous* sought to gain power thru
violent propaganda     down that *nous* it was old AHNÁHR traveled the invisible realm pro-
phetic invention which shaped the machine-age the historical arc then down to firing missiles
valorized by MOIRA     advent brought about medial range a beginning short-lived
nothingness totaled ruined evacuated the entire human empire from Earth     made way
for mesocosmics SEVLESMEHT realized in his pawning role after fullness the desert's horizon
*psyche* by which songs SHIRU would finally interpret and sing
THWIILASAQBẄ bridging fullness
the final Sophia     she in whom no attitude *projected* toward *idea* man
AVISTAVARZERVAIRYU     embodies     garment of light
interpenetrating origin perdurably

## *“Delay no more” *temps* replace World: Notes on the blackbird’s advice for the Quartet’s score

What end mystery un-seeking discernment of event?

MAN

dumb as a door-knob

“The special rhythms, independent of the meter, powerfully contribute to the effect of banishing the temporal.” M. *Composer’s Preface*

Apotheosis of one offspring into note lineage the Father encircles the camp with barbed wire heaven stalag-titic construction at the start near war’s beginning world begun thanatos undifferentiated milky utterance without touch
sin the capital by which its other manifests only in “revelation”
uncloaked kept the capsule of a joke
secrecy internment too slips into language the birds rising offal or burned off essence no longer any “use”

EARTH evolution of all wars
the very name of peace
posits spunk creation perversion which spreads out all spreading upward outward “speaks to us” instead of

. . . .

“non-retrogradable rhythms”

interesting most important to note Black Kali the appearance of just such a moment in adversity the very springs of created life itself

**so Xristos counterpart would be a falsity thus monstrous destroyer of life by his releasing war within a Logos as central generation of deathless MAN**

The note which descendants of saurian form sound contains **end** of MAN

we can hear however crossing tongue large throat out of which Kali spreads her tongue to lick up all false statement proposition contains an ever-widening uncontrollable multiplication of Lilith's substitution by way of EDN

the flip of the spread Kali rose to as Priestess of power chakras and circles re-involved MAN in celestial pre-substitutional apotheotic idiocy obsessive thought hearing and not-hearing as it thinks its unending the same as smoke's discharge

> "Whether read from right to left or from left to right, the order of their values remains the same. This feature exists in all rhythms that can be divided into two groups of retrograde related to each other by a "common value." M. *Composer's Preface*

Jesus the most common desire ever created: the wish to **be** God
takes polyphony by common stress (when stressed as total value translation of the term of delay in revelation alone not interactivations of circuitry pro-creative participation) spoils it in production of a look the entire embodiment of empire thus uniform

Black Kali comes to meet now over and over to rescue PLNIPLOI too in the mirror they both have never really seen but certainly heard the rumor of each in the other possibly in egg-shape of that non-retrogradable rhythm or span endangering even themselves

. . . .

## Abyss of the Birds

solo

flailing instrument to find the gate

Only SEVLESMEHT when he leapt into black fire    (hūp-ah!)

exhausted thru and thru by vaulted nothingness

his wish connected updraft toward one star

perfect timing rejoined new crystallization

seeing more than one before after black meaning's hold en-

cyphers

in its blackness

flue her tongue reaches thru his "head"

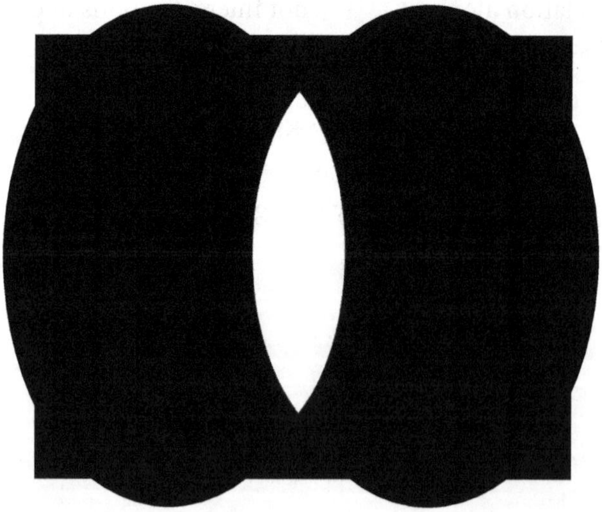

# After-Meaning:
# Messaien's Transposable Mode

In the sense of one composer's famous incarceration—made so from the composition he put into motion—internment translates our own time, whether it be at a loss to recover historical definition or even personal memorization; whether it is deemed to be competent or even a performance of this or that art, captivation still can be acknowledged. Acknowledged in the hope it might rise to the register of a recognition, the music played out from one group of musicians to assembled and condensed audiences.

*Quartet for the End of Time* was begun before Messaien's imprisonment by an invading German army that eventually occupied France (1940).

It is the recognition of two things at once, a palindromic (retrogradable & non-retrogradable) rhythm, and the Limited Transposition of pitch or scale which intersects with birdsong Messaien understood as the time signature to the composition. In other words, the absence of denotative time for a given bar of music was left out of the score. Instead, rhythms as well as pitch at the center of each movement allude to "impossibilities," limited scales and activities (forward as well as backward) of the composition in order to furnish a vocabulary that continually criss-crosses.

A limited or set group of musical components, repeating their own signatures as instances of their complete limit (much the same as a note is a complete and "finite" unit) makes the actual score funnel into the "abyss" of each of their occasions.

Messaien had already begun the score for what would become the central movement of the Quartet, "Abyss of the Birds," before his capture and subsequent imprisonment at Stalag 8A in Poland. So the idea of both a "serial" approach to building the language of a score and the phenomenal interface with birds and birdsong had already entered the composer's field of interest.

Could it be the blackbird, the *merle,* he had already identified with the space of a timelessness, is eternity itself?

It would be in keeping with Messaien's devout Catholicism that such a "transposition" would scale his own involvement with Xrist, as well as the world, just as it is found by each of us (on our own terms).

The intention inherent in the cross, then, is not simply a centerpiece to the "faith" of any one religion, as if it owned even the limited modes of its own understandings; rather, in those limited terms and vocabularies, those utterances, the eternal shows the listener the true meaning of doctrinal practice come to an "end".

In this use of an "end" (of time) everywhere, the various terms, incomprehensible by themselves, become completely understandable when inverted, turned around, made "retrogradable". (SEVLESMEHT).

# OOM
# &
# ONÖNYXA

Sun passage onto Earth's extant existent place magnetic void kosmic void the surface plain visionary Earth's face upturned galactic maw from which it first appeared out of dreams every population silly fervor manifests voices busy sounds below THERSEYN as he tracks his own path meridian voids winds both Erebus in Tartaros as well passage toward SHŌŌNWU now sees his own memory calling to compounded voices species forming isolated pronouncement strong signal forgetfulness marks the human anthropoidal nothingness a special deity they are compound into one chest radiates to planet's auroras he makes way out atmosphere pummeled by change in magnetics trajectory his version his own carapace to mimic constellation's Tortoise wriggling writhing purpose Snake bounding out of his cavity into tails tongues of Earth's reflective radiance Sun's hot magma starshine brilliance captivates tracking movement calendrical associations precessionary gathering all matter down he turns now because he sees ONÖNYXA in blank covering of Earth one whose tears can't arrive whose own passage stopped incessant shrill black garble of a species hell-bent on its own enfranchisement with matter where they do nothing but swell bituminous quarries surety breeding drinking black stuff until sockets in their skulls plugged they offer themselves to cycling scythe their own time not in sacrifice but glut blindness so THERSEYN turns on his snake-like motions un-sensed in Aetherial regions of oversoul ZAS family thru immense anti-motion of return makes way back into center the desert to re-write re-commence short-lived life expectant pregnancy left in same desert he knew worked to find passage as albumen of the planet sparks recedes he goes under horizon's lid it lifts lets him back in down to zero on cosmic form motion meanwhile herself slight emergency her center brings world back to its senses once again

OÖND occupied OOM occupied synaesthetic oneness any sides the era neither any way to come away overwhelming oppositions instead he'd contain flow til out either end whatever prevailed whole mental push pull became practiced push pull maybe too much everything began waste his world wasn't really his passed bequeathed everything to what protogeny do replicate give their birth to matter leap out lifetime's worth his matter reading thus all ejaculate immediate presence phenomenal world ZAS great progenitor does still wherever whenever he ranges

QAPTAKUSS figurehead image in on sand blown hardened language desert everyone thought this couldn't be happening so went reach something it wasn't there wasn't enough belief his reign inheritance left standing desert city pile-up sand archeologists talk about as if bait swallowed non-existent fishes in his beginning the empty desert unoccupied stands ersatz progenerator thru-out storied science embryonic mind mankind comes clutch thru vain epoch rendering incapacitation tantalizingly close threads biotic mania QAPTAKUSS bore in many-eyed shape only dreamed thru fitfully associative populations barbarity blood knows as if genetic key to re-descendence in a bath of unlawful gore shape uncontainable multi-limbed extrusion the worst of yet-to-be incarnations here as OÖND morphed and so called QAPTAKUSS

PLNIPLOI to encompass primitive wings new hyper-calculative bears births same status none more nor less than special emissary ambassador performs world thinking interpretation self dimensions at work insinuates his birth correspondence on off command superiorization of outcome by way head attached to mother MOIRA father ZAS out the pantheon temple to security sustainable prerogative a host of cells biologies the bios the vast ranges ZAS's wandering roving body forms clouds atmospheric seed tamed exuberance MOIRA incubates all bodily outlay relay circuitry the child PLNIPLOI

Fifth World prophetic character framed the entire ritual the city PLNIPLOI inherits even before named the City of Holes lived out story expanse desert ONÖNYXA went into that desert prophecy become future felt change toward lack of cycling re-cycling told continues be told background even now the Fifth World leading place vision's age or era time-span takes vision attempts re-place visionary it was ONÖNYXA changed brought the era prophecy to take pause emergent quality sound to pick up song kind of call SHIRU worked into world seduced AHNÁHR it worked down descent turned him caught essential shape his own spine echo reverb vibrates elemental creation EKSTONISTIAN descended thru song toward song SHIRU sang brought courtship AHNÁHR approached hidden Forest all the way into this also fomenting pool's water EKSTONISTIAN's base oneness the ultimate base inhalation sparks electrical wisps capillaried light where began the skull of THERSEYN

without song we'd have Fifth World PLNIPLOI his birth out of MOIRA ZAS source-code for war so SHIRU's seduction AHNÁHR brings new world thru reproductive ecstatic feeling-source arrays martial positioning AHNÁHR as well as THERSEYN makes way into constellation of SHŌŌNWU their inheritance out of clustering structure song flipping up for down and down for uprising sons of OÖND and OOM remain split even as MAN disappears from the face of the planet he an image alone the work Daughters ensure as image or stick-figure brought into channel their work the knapping stone we-aving of sighs with hands brought funneling winds ecliptic upsurge at OKEANOS threads sewn braided into rods ZAS at first but AHNÁHR whose return to deeper regions emanates the Forest floor he lay on EKSTONISTIAN the moment split and in the Daughters' show of hands fevered work to sacrifice send themselves ejaculation of all things shadows up into World-Tree the great precessional Axis-Tree the planet joined by work and as MOIRA ZAS trembled in memory the hope they saw offspring PLNIPLOI every mother father prayer into Daughters work became *total* sacrifice PLNIPLOI wished but not wished actively with all mental vacuity sent signal to overtake work turn it into further beheading fulfilling Fifth World's prophecy desert the desert's own signal sand an automatic vacuuming of wind and sand

Daughters themselves protean conception inception unconscious overlay apotheosis OKEANOS sends vision motion conflict turmoil the very nature of life mirror image two hands placed on the work shows image titanic does nothing but pass their station catapult image toward wobbling planetary Axis-Tree whose height contains essence differential life death material order work presents OKEANOS fostered giving work-place receives pantheon eventually understands if even momentary glance their own neither near nor far an activation site

groupings beginning herds packs hounds sent at one time to scour Earth turn it a Table-top come together in meetings have essential vibration essential code either war or cessation martial position body in graves bodies seen together the same pose position that thread OOM came to hear return ONÖNYXA who left with image of the father overlap mother OOM in so many overlaps echoic riches species felt ONÖNYXA returns thru desert but it changed in this the father too all artefactuality she took now she gave father see OOM see he not the cause of split in Sons the pantheon itself caused him grab his sense of power not larger sense this moment OÖND knew his role taken too personally MOIRA he had only concerned symbolic nature the pantheon not true cyclical celestial organization of power even now changing rotating constellations partially observed partially preserved mis-aligned signals in the individual human brain

Earth itself a synaesthetic return for which the entire species emerges awareness but eyes opening constellation northern contour interstice Ovoid shape commences eye not an eye any longer this or that assumption hasn't chance to see why deviciveness Earth planet as well as hands upon stone tools in paleo-identifications need come together into passage toward translation of Light so THERSEYN the backward step flight would help interpret light but controversy over subtraction sutures and the ontologizing of history even the least ratio of light reflexive analogy clouds with ZAS elemental ranging presence ensures static dream base to base in phenomenal the topological world

changes trans-positionings apparitions the pantheon played out again and again while song of SHIRU martialed spiny air the return of ONÖNYXA who brought OÖND out of QAPTAKUSS his city his prophetic hold upon the future as well as EKSTONISTIAN out the wild out the Forest not the Desert this change showed religion's too-much influence upon the State roles all necessarily changed for darkest passage toward OURANIAN curve ecliptic makes new constellation out of the word formation of a sword ages of human prophecy backward to secure similarity between THERSEYN and PLNIPLOI within World-Tree shape made unmoved a moment eternity shrinks to its true size inside funneling winds catapultations rocketing work Daughters perform at OKEANOS unity not of despair but exuberance all living things the incubation wells in their hands en route to farthest expanse opening time itself the folly of inner human plays out a used up image of themselves

THERSEYN then PLNIPLOI these creations sourced at different places in vast panoptic circling signals radio transmissions simple elemental configurations travel the atmosphere join weather patterns out of El Niño also buzz vibratory length leads us into OOM not so much out of stories although here and present the author typing away to keep up with wind rush became a block sometimes blockage the written word also the very sense time no longer and in that end of things presses down the human in human shape Animalia roused the split in Sons the primeval split the one most commonly thought biological anthropological but nothing further from truer pole plumbs depths history the pre-biotic organismal structure mineral wisps electrical availability downloaded into created cranium of THERSEYN done in such manner it took AHNÁHR to come back to this world seek EKSTONISTIAN impregnate her distance in the role he was summoned to play this far inhale sigh release brought about every other story the base song SHIRU formed first notes gathered the orgy for World-Eggs release them into each and every body the signal reason form solidified species to avail MOIRA ZAS likewise conceive at northern most borealis a counter child PLNIPLOI from all pressings joinings mergings and overlaps

out of vast structure seduction the body entered funneling winds the Axis-Tree toward SHŌÖNWU put there unitary action the work Daughters of AHNÁHR all the fingers work probe even unknowingly secret hiddenness EKSTONISTIAN who is the essence of the world of time and space destined conflagration the actual slippage Ovoid mirrorings of an entire species and into that Mirror they or some pass and this passage division of the cells division of the eggs place of entry aurora's seam toward constellations of darklight in Mansion of the Tortoise whose companionable Snake has two tails two ways to head two ways to have a tail this the relativity the entire field of spectral bodies even now make their way into sucking winds a verticality likened to vacuum the transverse appearance of matter itself and in the distance echoic features of QAPTAKUSS the vanity of OÖND who secured individuality of sight into a thousand violent realizations the two-fold realities of time and space yet by such all-seeingness lost everything so that his navel became one with the desert out of which emerged the older prophecies sacrificial blood-lettings the Fifth World re-sunk their teeth the soul of the City of Holes as if wind sand dust part of the unfolding time itself in semblance of one over-ruling fate

OOM the Ovoidal overlap presence first motherly humming ratio out of moan gestational round given bequeathed ONÖNYXA pure impartation from her parted open lips the Daughter's head emerged to view the world?

coupling OÖND the power elementally shared as to before after event records telling general reflexivity regarding coupling vanishes dries up or other metaphor to say at an end something begun but OOM no forgetfulness in this respect a special memory actually returns initiation site thus flowers plants the very nature of land any place itself made over by this return reality the first elemental sharing coupling this neither premeditated nor concocted trivialized connexion to coupling the phenomenal world moving from the world as thing relation we species into event why part the species extinct another becoming acquainted eventually surrounds everything OOM feels in her folds

death incoming hangs inside humans just as it does other genus other species but homo sapien rationalization turns death a very somber occasion symbolic associations attached never once acknowledging SEVLESMEHT eventually understand his smoke mantics screen all this tele-kinetics of the eye nothing whatsoever to do with brain they this understanding cease belief in future based on PLNIPLOI so wed to MOIRA cannot understand future but thru eye turns death absolute reason flat-lining imagination the species of course death-knell languages as well every symbolic treatise administered to sick healthy lame as well wise it's full-on mis-understanding of candy-ass treatment of themselves mockery toward every living thing seeks reduce to death-clutch leveled off apprehension as if born with hands no use the age of hands long past never anything be made by hand only eye death sign-language mutes given permission translates everything in a final dogmatic canine fulfillment of gesture

OURANIA the entire kosmos formed but it was at first over-riding sense of materiality ZAS wooed MOIRA became principle manifestation MOIRA insisted she model very nature a kind of marbleized piece of frozen lava met ZAS gas-born entity the two able have it all come off the pantheon then an appendage to them signal however from SHIRU some debate whether he was messenger composer of song turned AHNÁHR back from drift thru eventually far outside OURANIA whether SHIRU got it from EKSTONISTIAN first to be in labor this the overlap in human intelligence stories tell or make the same error telling OOM confused EKSTONISTIAN it's OOM gave birth to ONÖNYXA EKSTONISTIAN THERSEYN later but it wasn't birth SHIRU was singing drawing AHNÁHR back into Earth he knew EKSTONISTIAN hiding the only way he knew to radiate understanding her beauty superior intelligence within her hiddenness open his throat vibration timed to hidden abilities everyone knows goes high expanding adapting come to exapted sense the species itself knowledge the key acquisition essence bore the future she to involute down to bottom the Forest in this place insects Faeries exist able to tie breath enchant every form of existence become one with existent aroma wood itself this kind of thru-line ability cornerstone building block many nuclides and nucleic acids other atomic universals pedogenic isotopes protons mass of neutrons her memory gathers together SHIRU attempted mimic with song turned voice of time not so much story but meridian specter sensory feeling along spine of AHNÁHR history itself heard hunger source again roused AHNÁHR down thru the material world flew descent marking making new time outside previously known calendars myths cannot quite get at magnificence meaning this drive AHNÁHR traversed limits of Earthly dimension to get woman EKSTONISTIAN whose very embodiment called his own nature he was able reverse destiny cling to last shred of energy his essence down into her drove himself all the way thru down into ground actually the puddle at her base grew a pool in the Forest under canopy glistened mirrored the entire still regions the hidden copse that moment he came thru the other side de-objectified journey the same moment electrical connections in the pool incubated future skull one they talk in fossil records the cranium THERSEYN

OOM gave OÖND when first met very very early I'll tell the story only one time the only information obtained investigating sources two white stones OÖND one in each hand before her his upper body in fish shape a kind of pointy head snout black robe matching black belt took stones fixed them to his waist OOM sure she could see him made into dark distances surrounded steps where the Tree enshrined with dirt a voice moaned roots moving in the ground but OÖND a certain distant visage as if glowing stones tethered his passage in the world up to the time out in the night he to get into water could only be in air limited time returning to his own source hard to say but his time in upper air over he flopped down the edge the water OKEANOS whispering slid further along stones caught lip of narrow shore the lake or pond they slipped off his belt OOM saw sit motionless seemed eternity it didn't matter he wasn't coming back at least a changed appearance he returned no longer fish-top with only one eye but that was when she couldn't help took him into room just off main hallway fucked til ONÖNYXA created OÖND so full of himself this enterprise thought conducted engineered made manifest all that transpired so began grow more eyes til he tripping over bruising unable to navigate very well out in space took to cursing ordering servants until one day thought he walked thru Tree in the yard was the founding of his city transformation into QAPTAKUSS

passages into change of light day a warm glowing reminder entire Gloria the past then night obtrudes that same place becomes feeling transposed meridian outlay displaced concentrations light no longer referenced in the objective instead makes collective constellated relevance known thru different searching different seeking difference opinionated releasing self the hook-up belonging we see we flip out errant presencing whose one-sided dismissal of another side renders human ineffectual en route to extinction obviousness the hum OOM carries seed back into inceptual instinctiveness of first things matter reproductive cycles an Ovoidal passage

Sons of OÖND and OOM grew out of interactions many beings OÖND able to split off always ONÖNYXA missing from first must have been instinctual her reach took wand of OÖND without his knowing at the time such distracting clamor split inheritance Sons stood in front the big Ovoid Mirror debated she walked right into bedroom took the damned unit right off trophy case where enshrined by sign for STICK cross mark vertical mark joined to form right angle perpendicular future announcement first proven source city maybe even pantheon but that debate too she just walked away knowing eternity

fundamental difference EKSTONISTIAN MOIRA lies in each's relation to words all she can do to come out simplest utterance completely aware the momentary not so much a ticking time but place empty words that emptiness fullness her own travels length certainly breath existence so really manifestation breath itself this of course reason ZAS is torn between MOIRA and rumor of EKSTONISTIAN but MOIRA to ZAS immediately the follow-up plan in place immediacy has impact dynamic jointure anatomy itself joints articulate between maneuver another maneuver connections to Earth so blowing command into joint sure-fire way to get attendance maneuvering overwhelming echo physical motion even physical activation nothing to do isolation in history silence EKSTONISTIAN's great utterance the AH issued helped into out of furthest depth the penetrant AHNÁHR put seed of his syllable right to the very place THERSEYN began wisp forth atomic cranial weaving bone electrical marrow

separating OÖND ONÖNYXA brought change into QAPTAKUSS the sense of OÖND father never separated especially as into wilderness desert the most unused part OÖND to join reification the very essence herself manifest nearness possession the wand brought itself of previous name as image icon put into her own dense contemplations world the thrill its very seeming endlessness enough to water feed parts of her needed re-sapped not for nothing made her way out the City of Holes QAPTAKUSS busy cursing into shape spaces into lost ill-defined sense of Earthly time space would make her way into woods the pleasant mntn-sides leading down from plains outside the city adobe holes then more green aspects pine further then sand lines shore the land all formation needed encounter to match cancel his anger also the ability to fill gaping loss stagnation she knew to be un-natural ocean at last entire travel over those various landforms this birth her eyes finally oceanic splurge vast echoic strength dynamic relation to form her sex as well personal lineage began make her back armed with purpose symbolic OÖND given away this new attachment to wide-open universality inherent in thing seen known she to travel back backward movement her history knew marriage of all things rooted essential meeting not just token aspect men women but real insurgence every utterance as well every correspondence nature symbolic organization individual's lifespan as much part natural history Earth as her own span might take never to separate further this essence omnipresent to her eye

THERSEYN whether recognized or not at ONÖNYXA's side summoned there submitted to OÖND true nature surrounded OÖND that moment certainly summons essence of man it was ONÖNYXA to bring THERSEYN to place of submission the entire sojourn realize one correspondent to OÖND would be OOM thru whom return to self not so much return anything identifiable but return nature far off he gone in guise of QAPTAKUSS but possession of eyes ONÖNYXA's obsession reason commands such respect this whole pulling down around essence OÖND's relation power used unused world saw not so much OOM as plot-point quite the contrary she the element thread phenomenal wrap around throat SHIRU note summoned AHNÁHR submitted to seduction inside EKSTONISTIAN an enactment of what had been rumor now totality of one to one relations not the groupings of visions surrounding trapping each within dispensation from QAPTAKUSS the pantheon's interpretation as merely sight

Daughters given blood-test their sight and by this mineral compound makes anatomies perfect for work completely one with work reason they cannot be released from work otherwise would have the shape of rumor unformed story humanity by which to place themselves access work various controversies of age one the Sons in front the Ovoid Mirror as well inside Mirror the other shape rumor makes way in out of MOIRA's commands now been shown the very shape of childbirth PLNIPLOI proving material comfort ZAS provided by willing seed form of submission too makes its way all eventually clusters over Daughters at OKEANOS loud waters might carry in out various waves all the corners of the world just like form light in morning chasing capacity of darkness thru late evening

out of various sites rumors abound closer inspection bones used as tools perhaps gnawed upon always from them passage jointure anatomy skeletal vehicle sight brought brings passage toward whatever light available begins strike across planet brilliant eeriness could only mean never-to-be-contained essence in history of humans tho RED CIVILIZATIONS worked or try hunt what was hunt EKSTONISTIAN scattered into clans differences talk articulations only bring sight to rumor somewhere in rumor light just this second turned burning heat fuel rounding lip Earth to burn desert leaf-top canopied copse EKSTONISTIAN a plant somehow raises herself up toward view slipping head thru skin of green palms merging eye with patient expanse view intelligence synaptic revelation each every passage includes her being no matter where it might be arranged no matter the species shies away her strange length only engages essence stories curl themselves into woody vine small nodules knots on central Tree's trunk cling hold relay time after time

tribute paid ONÖNYXA when left City of Holes made way into desert flat plains endless land now known as Plains of AHNÁHR it was before this a risen specter washes over inhabitants as they to discern her leaving done and in that understand ways of production ways to harvest farm procure soil keeps moist cycles her disappearance her seeding firmament itself as if taken unused portions of Law turned into new Law seasons soil differently given increase as opposed to blind consumption fossil fuel ZAS passes over the City tries get his visage into new fecundity but the hidden sense the vast resource all matter tied up with prayers tributes to spirit of ONÖNYXA's theft

out the disappearance ONÖNYXA absolution of QAPTAKUSS became apparent supplications themselves insurgent repulsion previous rule that rule Law the world motivated to change overturn prevailing order even QAPTAKUSS swept lust for change it might be most seen heard where when most useful reorganization desire reorganizing City of Holes led errant discoveries all of which flew rumor-hold history humans began feel new prevailing everything new brings appearance ONÖNYXA from the very place she made her escape upon return was not coincidence but arrival return the Daughter alongside stranger semblance of male authority some sort really it was THERSEYN hodge-podge clothes things woven what he'd found on way up to enacting tribute ONÖNYXA to OÖND obvious the real change secured by QAPTAKUSS he changed shape thru door entrance passageway toward manhood why new always the entrance appearance disappearance as if a kind of re-beginning of what comes ends before cycles part of deeper turning away all circularity in search desperate search for facts ONÖNYXA not have returned if essence her revelation the nature of symbolization had not taken full root within the crossing larger area rumor become work would will engage her here on out now solidified beyond behind all events as if she knew absolute necessity her body over against other historical perversion interpretation moves in out the hidden seen in such a way creates consensus by unconscious means OÖND to be the one at the door this time

role OÖND plays only transmissive light of ONÖNYXA? only disappearance THERSEYN her strange other appeared she reappeared final pronouncement OÖND's existence? suddenly without much more than nodding off his own familiarity comes knowledge its possession everything within reach mirrors reach ONÖNYXA's one act tho other views scenes other acts yet to come moments in the past lived forgotten here they remember by her return see human eyes greater symbolic prayer deep into THERSEYN's disappearance or residence beside her withdraws specter-like from meeting place off out from knees another passage toward North horizon bending under Earth auroras divine intelligence hiddenness small sounds emit speech Father toward Daughter those wisps echoic to work his mind travel immense closeness distance his own birth glowing darkened captivity time created out of fullness openness emergence below surface the pool of EKSTONISTIAN spies his own source once again

place in time entire scope scale human histories gone come not just the blink of an eye but patient path story THERSEYN embodiment in question from moment he was brought into world til signal for this age brought need over all time space historical development this he neither is nor was really why disappearance all of a sudden Ovoid Mirror entire length breadth subject object all of it gone so long its shape evolved realization then in bleep a milli-microbial aberration of time proper time in general it disappeared Sons who standing before it now begin rumble roar such indigestion it's as if the entire world turned to series of disappearances as if nothing exists now where Sons of the interior if the Mirror gone where are rumors to issue if not Mirror there the Forest the fact all remaining soon-to-be-extinct gatherings have at least one last gasp they mean to use in pursuit over horizon of the moment

reproduction in light of disappearances quite obvious gone extinct this the moment productive capacities exceeding reproductions so voices now in crowds Mirror once stood self-proclaiming abdication of all things saying *it's over done completely done this is it must be some other reason at work besides this we've been had!*

Ovoid Mirror receives THERSEYN he is weeping immense pain unleashed movement translated into Mirror enclosure solidification all nights under lip of Earth there are others but all turned semblant creatures left over from productive drive the species the winds all up down cease to be horizontal effort living entities perceive within great overlap existence known as spacetime now funneling which was precessionary activation weather gone into center overlap where two contending winds meet repel one another one travelling in spiral up northern constellation SHŌÖNWU sucking vacuuming winds pulls those in overlap who understand downgoing nature time suck pull toward place of Erebus within caverns hollows of Tartaros subterranean place whose mineral airs carry all thrumming work Daughters perform somewhere thru-out its underground network eventually returns daylight eventual exits out of shadow up into land flung out force nature the re-constitution of ZAS whose very letter emblazoned onto unwilling traveler thrust into loam loess the Plains some landing headfirst others arms sticking down into pedosphere shattering bones in wrists as if bones were bracelets white stones white pebbles scattering into terrarium Earth

into other side Ovoidal Mirror creation matter knows no extinction immortal vestiges of souls shadow made leap thru Mirror down vacuum Tartaros up funneling winds Axis-Tree all in array two sides contained THERSEYN's chest the plastron Tortoise SHŌÖNWU whose inner snake two tails awakened wagged excitation at ultimate return EKSTONISTIAN's pool

every Daughter we-aving industriousness emblematic branding catapultation at OKEANOS desires find out sensory initiatives occur when break-out reaches adequate another Daughter or Son already passed thru Mirror this causes breathing with interior Ovoid in fact Ovoid shape itself pertinent used to break away OKEANOS this wishing these wants with those in Mirror align history at OKEANOS has for derived insinuation of ZAS so work stoppage finding historical OKEANOS not the real ongoing turbulence workplace caverns endless splurge rush up thru all this only snap picture icon this reason desire drives Daughters Sons back to work to sure clear measurements of any effort

out of his own chest to conjure safety ONÖNYXA secures pantheon in itself for itself out of might have been other age era all trouble buffeting realizes Snake etched upon plastron the form Mansion Night form the goal martial existence funnels World-Tree toward SHŌÖNWU to be carrier darkness endure shadows from Erebus take mantle of Tartaros within Ovoid Mirror gaze out from travel duality THERSEYN now makes in haste brain sweating urges flight close to ground where Sons look up from hauling wonder at this strange phenomenon now some leap into the Mirror THERSEYN intent on one form one essential forgetfulness the species conjuncted pantheon to mean tying together as returned double-headed creatures SHŌÖNWU to enter electric disturbance his birth echoing AHNÁHR entering EKSTONISTIAN

sons of OÖND OOM those who stay outside Mirror's passage deciding collectively material advances time space closeness every remote they've heard up to moment disappearance that moment the brain allowed finally function become one with Law inherent in things matter itself no other way they ever without this decision

OÖND complete his own time entirety of time history itself unity of self opposition OOM raised because extinction the species within completion OÖND returns to agency correspondence with Law missing ONÖNYXA OOM knows instinctually took his un-used part made it afterlife the new what new is without being symbolic representational fuel rumorous clouds atmosphere in house MOIRA behind visage OÖND this separation of OOM from MOIRA arrival of surrounding presences travels from EKSTONISTIAN's hiddenness all the way into this return meeting the pantheon place city out of which ONÖNYXA drew herself drew all rounds to herself to show species extinct the seeded instability of being extinct must recognize limitations the pleasure in this lives on in her even as THERSEYN seemed to disappear left her side even as she confronts mother OOM voice rarely heard but whose vocation in sight of throat presence ONÖNYXA echoes off time world also distance her voice to Earth ultimate presencing capability defining openness presence eventually leading existence toward precessionary activity World-Tree blending Axis-Tree a kind of musical tonality summons not only syllables but full word sound heard future to be this instant this cracked opened time

ONÖNYXA attracts OÖND manifestation of her essence allegorical channel upon which gods depend pantheon found will always find way toward open changeableness Law resides at back all things ONÖNYXA saw OÖND the symbolic register oscillating movement of time coming going this need this want herself this desire oscillation pole would be opposition to OOM opposition or difference of elemental self her utter self in ecstatic journey travels from home always the way sent within without the allegorical what Law sense climbing out of symbolic hollowness into openness of Earth thru her own pleasure thru agency aligned with Law magnetizing pole symbol come ecstatic ambulatory nature her life this place even acquisition Nations how they cease how materiality might lead in streaming defense offensive defend attack home always internalization Law isn't lawless this way by which ONÖNYXA moves the poem too the very nature Law composition Laws rooted umbilical nature defining reach the act of thieving taking the very seat all symbols exist in pretend disguise arrangement with power limited temporal alone this the thing she ceased grasped took herself in order the channel desire her own desire channel agency manifestation key the entire acquisition event meaning event works in world errantly as well as actually her mind image of images mirror in shape of rounded breasts she held knows in OOM they meet in return to allegorical charge forms the entire pantheon discharged thru change inner existence OÖND now re-inhabits out of loss visualization the world Sons of OÖND stand at the place the former mirror begins work conception motion central attribute to all things matter theory they attach to motion takes them into Aether they pull apart filaments of rumor encounter ZAS whole in trinity of family the entire history up to that point to re-visualize MOIRA beside ZAS baby PLNIPLOI sucking on all upward levitation at that point encounter Sons prophesized by theorems everything to all exists they need only find formula throw up out vast realism reason put into contraption this upper plane below astral night remaining mysteries they mean eventually vacuum thru PLNIPLOI's generation he is protogeny apparent calculative rendering EKSTONISTIAN completely absent from their world they remain nameless in this account until a further time in the future into vowel sounds ONÖNYXA passes they scoop into one-time world QAPTAKUSS they discern shape of allegory prophetic shape land was when she walked alone in aloneness the entire symbolic history mankind brought into her once again the reach to take OÖND and in that gesture was is quotidian resonance one step lone voice moving itself up into arrival of heightened sense every day entrance to future she sees this gift she gives herself now vowels tones her own speech her own reach come back shape the land future inhabited alone the entire city adobe structures the Fifth World gives way to structures of future empty plain upon which only remnants of RED CIVILIZATIONS and SEVLESMEHT trek en route somewhere other than home

sitting in the city of holes here adobe all around the very ears eyes ONÖNYXA gave to the world in order to save it from destruction this the Fifth World these very rooms she first sat before leaping out with talisman father's unused Law brought the desert as if the bed of Earth to find in that too she met ABRCLÉA then further back before that also loved THERSEYN in threesome act of dirt green alertness able to find in her own tracks animal tracks ears eyes her own being far reaching potencies the nature of Law cyclical laying actual ground in ground learned raise to the night in morning sun became moon by which she met ABRCLÉA joined embrace brought her all the way to ocean rumor rose above the world because her journey that same rumor consolidates holiness all rounds redounding efforts might have existence within Ovoid Mirror from this same journey sacrifice an offering her heightened alertness a once voiceless creature shapes the age we live eyes ears we hear with now

what are would-be thoughts striking the world ONÖNYXA ranges Nightsky in search of herself to find first essence the kind of coming once again also rumor of EKSTONISTIAN at this place rumor herself coalesces with natural sky ZAS no longer quite evident Nightsky gives idea world how much time to come to positions self selflessness why so desired OÖND even when it might have been taboo might have been Law broken instead Law vision enlarged enlarging world or this enlargement solely her own senses dilating inner revelations inner revelations reflective world she bore in history to allegorical spanning thought it is also thoughts arranged in similarity EKSTONISTIAN out of THERSEYN she first heard saw arrangement EKSTONISTIAN a body so unlike her own mother but only story shape story come go be as it doesn't plan be twists turns sometimes happens also say speech comes not so much from person one teller but an aggregate maybe hooking up same seeing same televisionary channel like SEVLESMEHT wanted become one with tried so hard to see smoke his fire later abandoned smoke became fire isn't that ONÖNYXA feels she sees essence EKSTONISTIAN never met her seen her only heard about great hidden goddess in forest the most hidden place in the planet?

EKSTONISTIAN's presence looms birth death-site wandering insight mindfulness ONÖNYXA sees ability in rumor more than rumor presence neo-calculative agency world whose various stations move upper to lower shrink extend light plumb darkness positions homo sapien to places they wish find thru roping formulae mathematicals MOIRA's view pantheon to attention tableau projected limited totality whereas EKSTONISTIAN's reach similar to ONÖNYXA's discovery symbolic at an end what comes next fulfillment length breadth skin bone thrown up over world where even now catapultations out of OKEANOS send refinement above Earth ONÖNYXA sees firmament electrified captures essence of ZAS-borne emblematics Daughters some fall back to Earth re-acquainted perhaps with atmosphere as if objects memorabilia given AHNÁHR's re-emergence in Aether signal direction thru passage funneling winds issue precessionary Ovoidal Mirroring empictured extinction of the human

PLNIPLOI heir to the entire pantheon armed with will assurance MOIRA has seen return ONÖNYXA reappearance OÖND interprets changes entrance of the new out of which PLNIPLOI will emerge the truest most enlightened she hunts pantheon its halls once again looking every secret mysterious passage to turn any all clues the history forsaken whatever else might make case against PLNIPLOI her son the golden one mother's a marbleized adamant pillar perpetual promise out of image visage ZAS towering substantial history pervades all other histories calculative influx inflexible views toward entirety the planet in northern borealis MOIRA chose the spot dedicated passage into realms mansions above horizon Earth a place by which deposit her child circling sometimes dizzying perspective human history as the sun rounded out green fingers auroras he was presented in splendor her placenta divinatory combination to all locks the new presented the world evolves or devolves or simply each a stage knows her son willingly prepares grown from that one entrance exit site of the planet

voice the center her eye ONÖNYXA begins sunrise all other voices merit this eye this one voice can't be heard right in center the moment would speak ray out over what thought disappeared chased away by light claims this place planet again movement meant for her to find seek sojourn take EKSTONISTIAN out from hidden place but how could she be so presumptuous it doesn't matter maybe she can take into pool the Forest find skull its history maybe she won't find but that place toward now in waves of temporal wisdom unlike any before she stores her body like never before

everyone ONÖNYXA said farewells to OOM entire population lived vicariously thru her to witness correspondence all families within one family on steps the pantheon's entrance ONÖNYXA dressed in traveler's clothes looked up the crowd then OOM in distance OÖND feelings welled as moments to gather mortality her own capability saying anything made words sound like they weren't written for something important this goodbye which would last forever longer than the pit of her couldn't draw anything more than sound her words falling into mortal gathering these people lived vicariously thru existence another plane another world really just out in places weren't here wasn't fair to them consciousness should have two-fold relationship she began put words together knew capable to draw out agencies populations in her chest breathed out blew words recounted her life beyond adobe city how pantheon so far from thoughts but alive in everything as long as eyes ears see hear she even saw animals telling all now even animals reminded her relation home to parents OOM OÖND then everyone looked at each other for animals other's eyes ONÖNYXA stepped down from steps to ground the moment the singing of SHIRU reached them or ONÖNYXA alone enabled to hear him

MOIRA seen heard too ready takes entire human race out splits their heads open analyzes contents reads prophecies her own gestation every nook cranny see hear how her term of time with other of a place time continually vexing every head the tell-tale signs this vexation without merge without birth without her destiny THE destiny isn't any other reality even the possibility another she has always only lived one birth not the other had one child born of one womb never any except her own seed from ZAS *ah!* suddenly alarmed *that damned husband of mine ZAS seed how it has to be that seed or was another in his seed or more than one that's it!* out she flies over the world into cloud contains father of PLNIPLOI confronting him re-arranging his features to examine essence does this and peers down thru break in clouds they both moving over the AMAZON endless river surrounding green mist coagulates moisture frozen Aether back into view occluding vision

THERSEYN's bounding thru world not stuck nor alive is alive passage sought he found overlapped with human frames onward into cosmic cycles historical verisimilitudes want him or any for that matter out of step with divine in step with human struggle issues contrary winds in middle the Ovoid Mirror where funneling winds lead Axis-Tree whose main growth patterned 26,000 year return of planetary focus every single day

if pantheon not allowed evolve emerge its own investment in itself not just the entire world Earth it might have secured AHNÁHR in shape of OÖND but was motion history so become everything gods to have one not possible as AHNÁHR heard song SHIRU brought position seduction not really oneness or unity himself over everything rather spirit of history called this sense wanting desire in strong history essence historical realization himself become one oversoul called him back to atmosphere Earth matter thru matter essential ingredient SHIRU passed thru throat into supernal realms AHNÁHR almost completely disappeared turned turning a driving force wanted understand hunting EKSTONISTIAN the same he might gather up all rumor dislodge from Earth knew he had to go into her most hidden essence was is essence history evolution pantheon drove thru matter to get her in doing contained all acts extensions in EKSTONISTIAN all the way hiddenness he was exposing place on Earth remained unexposed so to preserve place lowering emanation electrical disturbance THERSEYN light starry flicker meridian immensities pool EKSTONISTIAN created by her own desire to hide below surface just below time space itself emergence a skull out the formation bone cranial captivities currents AHNÁHR's descent brought entire being THERSEYN his tongue contacted terminal end of AHNÁHR as well the most hidden zone of EKSTONISTIAN

PLNIPLOI in full possession his head knows ONÖNYXA how she conquered desert Plains of AHNÁHR doesn't worry him deep in corners eyes will find his own history part of the legend of her will be when things too late when he has run out of time in the meantime plenty stokes time his mother MOIRA and out ONÖNYXA's mouth words names continue issue she walking further into world time space traveler companionless not felt alone but journey discovering root source languages within herself echoic nature sound atmosphere light comes elemental attachment of thing to word names rung depth of her journey now out from pantheon in search what world next as if discovery happens an elemental echo in atmosphere as if Earth resonance meaning hence holder of light chased darkness shadow semblance of things to edges beginning reality of light was more human sight attached to not thing at all but size shape every particle creation scaled by available Light she is history species embodied this constant journey back forth now aftermath showing OÖND to OOM revealing OOM open mouth sounding out to light animality surroundings plains various creatures appear in light defined by light she names appearance power moment issuing from mouth connection Fifth World embodiment had to form her own giving back to very place she took single symbolic disuse from once again putting existence into form of light as if prophetic sense continuation futures out of pasts never knew more nor less than her this wandering has to take place world wandering search EKSTONISTIAN for which tones vowels now in full releasing themselves out of elemental mortality rounds out essence tracks in dust by which coyote canine wolf pack presence searched over terrain she sees utters moment out loud exposes everything in desert moment then passes into atmosphere of extinction homo sapien all this time her own prints followed by MOIRA has sensed this presence sniffed anatomy of time wandering creature looking to conceal every trace throwing down onto scene her husband's corpse anew it is ZAS MOIRA throws night in the form of forgetfulness ONÖNYXA wakes in middle the darkness as if surrounded by alien shape her own being lost in pitch black ONÖNYXA listens to distance where distance the giving-way space supposes thinks it is as thoughts like stars attempting divine a Nightsky

MOIRA before Sons outside Ovoid Mirror makes her case pretty simple if they wish secure their side the Mirror's reflection into eternity they need PLNIPLOI in their sights fix him otherwise the various murmurs making way out of OKEANOS the round of history begins repeat itself will find Daughters this time engaged in AHNÁHR and his big turn-around re-entry into atmosphere of Earth story will replace other stories so Sons of OÖND then and there pledge do and MOIRA makes away from them all eyes on her backside sway entrance as if appearance of time itself they signal one another begin pick Mirror up where it lodged in Earth and as they move to get a better angle PLNIPLOI's reflection to catch just then rumble heard out in phenomenal aggregate of sound horizon of the world out of the West darkness falls upon mntns distance swallowed by stars returning constellations ONÖNYXA feels existence left with the returning Nightsky without one memory to orient toward phenomenal appearance of available light under world at passage to SHŌÖNWU cycles rebirth their view illusory extant length breadth of things day ends night comes on day returns still passage the various souls locked in world given entrance into under-horizon the horizon Earth phenomenal passage Ovoid Mirror contains voice the passage and the winds funneling updraft once again along meridian expanse of lights toward martial array of stars forming distant goal where all eventually discharge release from waiting resistance acquiescence all orders an extinct species their dream that hasn't begun

Now the Mirror darkness an obsidian cast turns to stone Sons in their effort sweating to move they begin to see in it Daughters taking edges of stone tools flame out their hands edges of the Mirror knap into razor-like rounded cutting implements as if Sons given this vision movement of the Mirror continues already in unconscious assimilation the Ovoid picks up edges sees blood draining their own hands begins jump back in bellyful curses back lets the Mirror fall to Earth where swallowed covered landslide from distant mntns whose totality nearer than thought what agreed upon in spatio-temporal collectivity their cabal

absolutely no time to waste now the prophecies the Fifth World set in motion over head of ONÖNYXA she it is took entirety of all cycles calendrical associations which end in murder taken them upon herself the weight dark night itself proof THERSEYN enters the tiniest ray of light comes bounding over rim of Earth puts himself into kosmic nothingness to investigate Law of one world any and all other worlds so begins communing tele-pathic passage thru inner depths of the Mirror for ONÖNYXA translation of the pantheon too far? or is ONÖNYXA always too far only carrier the species to such degree it incubates or needs incubate what she provides protection this not part of anything but transit translation becomes calendar OURANIA becomes Fifth World becomes any of the elements that move in Nightsky ultimately fulfills destiny the human within self person that moment again helps into afterlife species by way of a bridge or token any specks of light stars in bigger story years calendrical associations history brings brought collectivities toward realization their future only here in desert she knows feels pressure distant mntns press now on as the entirety of human endeavor but she has forgotten anything it's not the species sought gain dominance over her but fact mntns now inviolate assertion of any all futures their peaks she sees little flashes concording birth sight as if for her alone as if element of sight alone her entire life moves up into limb her lifelimb her bodied embodiment now moves into forgetful passage out toward horizon

sensing THERSEYN's movements in the phenomenal world ZAS's eyes awaken moment the noose-shape existence appears to his son PLNIPLOI who has the containing seal signal complete shut-down given to himself by cloak of night enters that cloth that warp weave where open eye everywhere shuts knowledge insinuates himself along walls opening essence large edifice built by Daughters flung out from OKEANOS all the rods emblematic we-avings of the temple of ZAS now make a kind of mansion on Earth because of AHNÁHR's re-entry all of this possibility now PLNIPLOI's means to an end manufactured for so long took his being born from MOIRA whose blood cellular charge creates the coming together egg and sperm matter for perfection human form now in perfection of form summation of knowledge takes over edifice many passages resounding one pattern escapeless dream a kind of corralling urgency in human shape trajectory centering on ONÖNYXA has ability to shut the beginning down cap tight restrict her movement to this scene alone her eyes ears limited complete in evolution that difference in her being to being before historical verisimilitude OÖND OOM emergence of QAPTAKUSS the City of Holes all of it nothing more than itself in ever widening circles amnesia of the new shows in her own willing submissiveness to the rounds of her body high by the highland mntns stoned out of her mind for the entire species

between surety and doubt THERSEYN exacts moment into effulgent patterns his own birth out eventually thru time passage mounts SHŌÖNWU martialing essence leaps into woven pattern night woven ensnares effort of ONÖNYXA so that not even out of pity his chest takes the new emblem of Tortoise sears his own chest in the snake with two tails upon himself downgoing thru atmosphere resonates essence of SHŌÖNWU this leap all could be got of the future neither correct nor seen stems from AHNÁHR into world his own turn this now this leap THERSEYN into night was what void took as vocabulary his own birth from tongue now into snake plastron inevitability ribcage entering atmosphere making fragment all space enlarged memorialization no longer simply function or mechanical attribute categorizing time and space this then playing playfulness can wake Law requirements ONÖNYXA begins not only see lights moving in Nightsky night itself trajectory she recovers starts investigation encompasses not just desert but terrain now free and open security not only memories but those lodged in shut-down stalled will the only deliberation her sole existent mere semblance of shadow PLNIPLOI's desire serious non-debatable region of matter his only fuel for shut-down she meets in a cataracted moment of human pathos

connection to Daughters and AHNÁHR's visit as if in moment one interlude eternity all time co-branded ZAS's presence now THERSEYN surveys walls of the house how he got turned from path passage toward SHŌÖNWU out of Ovoid Mirror thru Axis-Tree here now he knows this house Daughters work sends up a kind of signal of light from catapultations illuminates house as if night reflection SHŌÖNWU his own destiny now Earth-bound circulations fingers work over we-aving at OKEANOS and those sounding thrumming thrushes their work those rods ZAS imprints land in dirt soil planet with every intention THERSEYN reflects within unused portion ONÖNYXA to turn matter of the planet into precessional destiny why things arrive whenever they will some on time some delayed aspect it is THERSEYN gone into translation of night blackness of no light to translate eventuation of all motion picks up forgetfulness ONÖNYXA taken thru biopoesis ONÖNYXA the essence of work consonance Daughters who labor what to commence unfolds in the house OKEANOS blackest night faint presence AHNÁHR motivates entitlement ONÖNYXA thru THERSEYN by virtue of his own turnout funneling winds Meso-Near into Earth in blackest darkest night his double-tailed snake to light Tortoise's constellation show martial rear-guard time appropriation destiny ultimate essence souls now THERSEYN the mansion of Earthly Night

here the emblem phenomenal world under ZAS and MOIRA their son PLNIPLOI transpositioned double-tailed snake of THERSEYN forgetfulness of extinct species homo sapien brought away from false memory into true consideration the fillip buttress relation walls house electrical current runs from historical facts the beginning of time to re-wired circuitry stars fall from supernality for ONÖNYXA recovered by snake with two tails each of unforgettable moment taking the entire prophetic even at sacrifice of her own past to plunge out of the heights and into Earth

ZAS franchised Daughters at OKEANOS? anything else would seem to be an edge vertiginous monster identity calls into rumor shapes pantheon humans to suss out by patented process itself become from first engine MOIRA's truth foremost could be framed thus the question of ownership MOIRA by way of Daughters surprising everyone such a group could assert never having come to committee

THERSEYN wears the course of human destiny has taken stars out of Nightsky placed in house his return atmosphere Earth emblem generations will see hear long to crawl out consciousness toward Snake with two tails awaken this desire will hear rumors if that maybe not even but will in some sign perishable sign sputtering remnants of THERSEYN adhere psyche human if he has a psyche in the future if even hold such a thing all doubt the species extinct of necessity so it is a voided heart-throb THERSEYN experiences as he comes into Earth's experience for dead dying death animal rationalis but so he has instead snake constellation SHŌÖNWU all of this because ONÖNYXA treads forgetfulness her own form to find far edges now making toward Forest rumors issue or at least hearing her own its own history expunged all others so phenomenal really now only seen heard vestiges various calls activities activations light dark measured newly so out those calculations differentiations animal mineral distant workings the Sons try move Ovoid Mirror ONÖNYXA see hear this they try move creature maybe goddess certainly deity power but she has no memory except this new sense dark light sprung in her so name out of space lungs heart plods along EKSTONISTIAN begins issue out beyond mntns just now rising upland onto

phenomenal world renders human history obsolete MOIRA to look for ZAS enters Aether one more time to penetrate the very core what incessant need to keep tabs on Daughters why they have any bearing whatsoever with order she and him and PLNIPLOI by generative capacities expert manipulation the entire destiny the pantheon but there a large open gaping the Ovoid Mirror stands looking straight thru ZAS right into MOIRA a blinding flash of light *God damnit! Why are you so fucking porous?! We're going to have to do something about all this light shooting across the Nightsky into our lives it's making a mockery of my voice even as I speak!*

humanity now into THERSEYN future perpetual so by this the double-tailed snake real unreal captures entire interiority mirrors reflexive glance Ovoid Mirror taken by winds the other side passage vacuums Erebus in Tartaros stony existences are and not make way to OKEANOS thru underground passages up into working hands Daughters circulating all this water Earth wind flashing light one solar power incubates these things taken into THERSEYN Sons continue argue limited specter cognitive faculties refuse the phenomenal destined argument inaugurated bowels of history produced MOIRA the being of truth ZAS the world included in winds bellow blow as if the lie the shaping truth in longevity every passage to the floor the moving yet immobile Mirror

Sons dragging Mirror cross land when already proven thru many reflections reflexivities of light possesses parameters triangulations the world regardless what they think whether known or traveled imagine Ovoidal shape contour gives out radiation radiance beauty not simply still image picture frame but power of powers shapes Earth they ride source fuel unlike gaseous Aetherial carbons fuel Sons relations in RED CIVILIZATIONS but if they understand this admit connectivity over so ineffective it might as well finish some other cause be run with but cause to do Mirror moving here to there embeds labor sweat physical rotundity the Mirror economy does not really need does not need be concerned with interior so world maneuvers this work transporting it cross land

how utterly ignorant Sons those Daughters still blind split infinitives side with rumors RED CIVILIZATIONS destined for order amongst humans completely extinct and haven't begun think with ears nor Ovoid Mirror processed this double beat from the World-Tree shows passage to SHŌÖNWU into not captivation Mirror but winds to SEVELSMEHT found smoke manticisim a lone being from the herd allowed see own to jump into fires transit open realm AVISTAVARZERVAIRYU hiddenness revealed a secret history the species legacy THERSEYN discovered thru sucking winds martial positioning SHŌÖNWU to AHNÁHR's descent his birthplace now THERSEYN reacquainted can only track as he returns descends atmosphere here now figure ONÖNYXA embodied lost capacity herself in place of her own population movement return of her own father by shape she took into journey transiting essential everywhere signaled emergence thru stories history all gatherings

how Mirror essence water since THERSEYN came back Earth birthplace his desire to be with ONÖNYXA is birth pool EKSTONISTIAN ONÖNYXA makes toward density hidden sense shows thru night this stripping bare memories to newer memory truer memorialization thru mortality her guts listening immensity day night for EKSTONISTIAN ambit of time history unconsciously harboring destination in form EKSTONISTIAN hearing Goddess by edges seeing horizon longing to be her safety her place stars now newly moving Nightsky she sees not so much shine but light taper re-positioned drop by drop immensity measurement not just sentimentality but actual travel kosmicity she so dearly loves primordial conjures her viscera

do Daughters by ZAS have memory of THERSEYN do they recollect or is work all for glory of MOIRA to prepare the future for PLNIPLOI make sure land replete with catapultations rods out of we-aves at OKEANOS a natural ability within nature naturalness every act embedded into land each of these catapulted rods letter Z sewn into shaft sown into soil stand monuments to one desire which runs circulation never slippage toward Sons of the Mirror's interior never tremor trembling might recall THERSEYN before he began toward SHŌŌNWU?

Sons drag Mirror over land law defined sharpened for no other to secure entire place of all projections Daughters sense what happening out of OKEANOS a natural right its own destiny works Sons the work Daughters join fastening fascination with possible eras out of rumors from nearly extinct RED CIVILIZATIONS but this organizing principle the other side the Mirror no basis upon which a future place so Earth becomes prime importance Law must maintain scribe into place sentimentality as well sober realities time and space subordinate to commands dictates of MOIRA she gathers ZAS's length thru-out the world brings PLNIPLOI his next meal a hit from strongest pharmaceuticals the pantheon groans under weight of its various imaginations

could even one organization one Nation found of loose network of extinct beings organization even to realize parameters light dark make way toward interior the Mirror see larger features thinks the future delivers immortality no longer possible this mortal feature this extinction back to the very first Paleo-far rears itself in Meso-near descent by which large small made way thru kosmos constellations fallen houses mansions of night all these centered opening never planned for EKSTONISTIAN first in intuition all the ways up down in out species traveled worked suborned elevated she knows within movement height the canopy roof the hidden Forest to pool at her base the same AHNÁHR plunged returning essence to give capacitated electrical disturbance THERSEYN's form his cranium consonant universal bearing apogee turned perigee thru precessionary axis World-Tree back into Earth it was SHIRU sweetly singing told the passage primal translator for EKSTONISTIAN's hidden place

ONÖNYXA has begun climb reaches altitude in distant mntn range close her breathing intense sees slight passage looming juts incline makes way with limited memory one opening imagines many more suddenly the possibility falls on her turns to vastness her own prospect seems not awareness Earth disoriented depths the view a face or kind of face gathering energies animal human creature two faces one disappearing the other great distance she feels nearness toward aperture the mntn entrained to the first approximation her own species sedimentary actual nothing encountered before at this climb opening suddenly a fissure the ground opens stops in steep depth too much now sit wait meditate figure the light leaving or soon this time stillness brings on sleep

Sons measure distance progress dragging Mirror across land ONÖNYXA sleeps dreams abyss over oceanic radiating immensity time space this traveling cell to cell communication Faery realms echo blood-stream into crevasse issues shadows Erebus as Tartaros emitting great black cloud crowds atmosphere dream upper reaches the world ONÖNYXA travels shadows electrical currents house Mansion THERSEYN out of return into Earth dream turns two elemental lights circle disks eggs cross in sight then blinding electrical disturbance universe looks down thru her feels THERSEYN voice naming shadows out of Erebus out of Earth two eggs light uncross separate each traveling separate orbits disturbance in blood wakes her as if stirring how memory from this doesn't matter but quaking disturbance tongues jolting essence not herself all awake doesn't have a clue but knows everything sees touches legacy of her past

without weight of history event completely invisible awareness history doesn't any phenomenal THERSEYN toward host anatomical relativity not acknowledged eyesight humans never tested determined concerned only when Mirror moved so mechanics all synched to other machinations yet the very air THERSEYN's chest swooped observed by Sons Daughters light change it but some inside the mirror inertia of his speeding heightening universal sexual matter elucidate electrical disturbance to which re-enters now glaring omniscience time capricious divine wrested planet every inhabitant partners global limited diabolical parameters brought PLNIPLOI's rundown capacity up into neo-cortical matriculation enzymes gaseous flares colorless odorless vapor ZAS's traditional repartee out of El Niño meeting eastward movement before La Niña changing paradigm of prophecy itself

Law broken abolished the moment AHNÁHR made way toward seat source forgotten even by himself to go into dark void destiny in returning toward EKSTONISTIAN codes based on insane interpretations completely misunderstood principles Light now stands in place waiting to be instated words all signs bled from sap World-Tree radiates black incisiven Forest EKSTONISTIAN that place AHNÁHR saw lightning stoke source creation chemical OOM pantheon's charge OÖND surcharge power turned City of Adobe administrative assumptions pantheon without foundation without overlap wanderings of sedentary mind QAPTAKUSS became alien extinction where even now mass graves without trace populations dug from Earth exposing massive fraud last-minute exodus

ONÖNYXA as the end of historical basis in Law re-instigation kosmic recapitulations self-sacrifice undoes the very nature of obedience teachings letterings all of it undone the Fifth World prophesized arrives erased in exodus the City of Holes chased out scattered into night blending Nightsky each leaping Ovoid protection the Mirror kosmically re-envisioned whereby gods see-thru lucent merge with light so Law itself ONÖNYXA's reach to take OÖND his unused self invest existence in devolution discovers ecstatic thrall forgotten part her species OOM to circle now brought essence reproductive capacity overlap to give way interior Mirror human imprint matter out of which emerges not one world but two

evolutionary spectacle Earth's inhabitants transformation Meso-near given passage the Ovoid Mirror changeableness strife abundance of matter whereas Paleo-far given Land sedentary dwelling continuity either-or brain PLNIPLOI's employed for neo-opposition meaningless fictional a sway persuasion no resolve even in reflection inhabitants especially they preen not poke liquidity surface Mirror stand boredom benchmarks of labor brings understanding of time so isolated from time only PLNIPLOI embellishes discerns meaning into either-or he owns maintains relations articulation resolutions interpretive guises emanations within time of Earth even as precessional guarantees release passage at northern extension of the planet makes way each and every day issuing souls releasing martiality of SHŌÖNWU as close to essential THERSEYN double-tailed snake universality of matter proper measure under one Mansion in deep space other Mansion Night whereby living ONÖNYXA vehicle transpositions within without flex and flux galactic milk rains thru him now races toward her they merge and all prophecies to change every future coupling capitulation confronting their existence within one another's essence

Admission emission come to one another great evolving devolving species hooking the very place his birth ONÖNYXA entered the grove to face EKSTONISTIAN tho she isn't apparent but in this place this one hidden the very wellspring at back of history transposes nature security not knowing but returning exuberance electrical disturbance in mankind consonance to resilience no matter size shape always extension even in visible invisible ONÖNYXA stands in presence completely alone thunderous exposition air makes way density AHNÁHR travels expenditure of light thru wood down into pool the outline of EKSTONISTIAN ecstatic shape shown in furthest depth just below surface the pool she creates rising out of THERSEYN takes completion of his form up to this moment history the world unborn thus the pressing drive AHNÁHR claims primary thru all things thus EKSTONISTIAN brought from her pool's divine creation into THERSEYN brings ONÖNYXA into hidden essential incubated time

pantheon resonates beating fire animations presences gone the gamut lesser greater by closeness distance signal in every stage or age world now to ground return gods to ashen Earth whence they began burning sending essential personages into Ovoid passage circulations from central Earth Law now kindled forged fire blood effected in its banked adytum touch prescience vista sparks ascend atmosphere divine shapes a future world whose underworld one with overworld time space also forever write space and time

here now the pose THERSEYN takes ONÖNYXA into animated stillness from the course of events her recent past of all pasts absolute aknowledgement sameness positions attend entire Earth this also moment electrical disturbance stories various ways elucidating letter transpositions diacritical flushes handmarked pages constitute compounding disturbance in electrified body THERSEYN embraces opens ONÖNYXA to place embodiment omniplacing over time to find the very seed-coil unravel it ravel it inexhaustible inspiration two rapt immobile motilities the very first stage the very first pose the very first transit cross horizon ecliptic infinity dim brain of humankind cannot even in this second lovely arc of pleasure fathom connectivity two entities flowing completely into the other ONÖNYXA taking the planetary beginning of all beginnings THERSEYN pulls his head feels his tongue rattle juices his talking various overlaps ONÖNYXA's naming agency charges dilation moves animating emanation THERSEYN meaty spit-filled glottal continuity of cognate sound as well identifications stream shared consanguinity Law freed blindness limited history extinct species given descent protonic non-relative phenomenality its power no longer dictated by earless prophetic THERSEYN ONÖNYXA arch themselves empurpling compact future announces out of primary radiation of the planet two beads phosphorescent ONÖNYXA's dream come announce presence in form of wheels each wheel into the other somehow two by virtue doubling glow merely shown to be concordance duality the nature of all singular things

loudest thunder opened in canopy above EKSTONISTIAN appearance descending high lightning AHNÁHR crossed through worlds to get this one doubling beat his heart transposed out of era gone sense of Law proportion comes to an end all of it to superstitious confined nonsense a deaf world his disturbance caresses the entire length EKSTONISTIAN's living resemblance passage phenomenal charge each and every conference sacralized THERSEYN's own doubling passage thru ONÖNYXA's sweet fundament

OKEANOS surge brought Daughters the doubling command to work MOIRA's afraid of in minerality their caves for the most part left that inspection to ZAS now turns to PLNIPLOI investigates two-fold apparitions make their way into the world have made world over Law seem as if written by an idiot she can't believe what PLNIPLOI will inherit she is worried extent unwieldy knows everything taken care of by brain of PLNIPLOI but all loose ends how they might be within historical record so sets to work to ensure Daughters never question Sons continue dragging weight the Mirror cross land these activities ensure backward looking glance sees nothing of collapse the pantheon instead will turn steadfast flatline uncreative firstborn PLNIPLOI she begins make tracings capillaries standing out from his young bald head framing them in her hallways until the main exhibit museum how long did you think for future to fall apart or had you much hope it would prophecize you now gazing as if this the projected sends ahead establishes historical same goes into bones now they dry un-Earthed without scrape of marrow if that world once lived were fantasy traces you as they nothing but part of a species in margins footnotes while real written out of every insubstantial contemporary trace you are extinct only a slippage reflection to see

EKSTONISTIAN's pool everlasting eternal Law brought threshold creation the same source code to other seed in this speech straightening royal occasion advent out of essential soft glistening reflection strong undertows lineations interest beyond mere seeming material enfranchisement rules collected meted sight or command these words written in swift water fire longs mightily thoro-going understands principle shout urge flame more than enumeration tally or box of matches whose game determines for all time legitimacy claims water gold out of dark night pool shines beyond accumulation wealth is part of Earth a part seen the entire Earth made hidden feature Angelic echoes the pool itself a cry heard in densest realization all changed

surveillance neither totality nor path leads feast glutton wants every sight conform every silence rest ending word by tongue THERSEYN actuates his crossing down into ONÖNYXA by virtue of her apex human forgetfulness human time slippage in out itself THERSEYN lets his own loose correspondence swim billow in her sway grazes surface pool knowing entire world entire universe his transit thru her mind place overcoming sequestered identity plain simple constellations move Mansion SHŌÖNWU thru THERSEYN milky light shines inter-animation ONÖNYXA at bottom of EKSTONISTIAN's copse hidden detritus every rotten composted thing so very mention of Law moves transit sets degrees planetary motion measurement THERSEYN this act summons into ONÖNYXA's creation into abilities possibilities all of them lost ready accept his emission as pilot accepts vehicle maneuver from lift-off to landing we hear EKSTONISTIAN's forbearance give way discharge her own developments to live here in the Forest Law itself un-Lawful adherents neither hear nor see same applies as far as each faculty unfolding revealing nearness trunks the trees so Faeries come tiniest animated presences preservation memory Forest their own stories acted performed pantomimed situations show silliness human species also other Animalia now gone into wood deep recesses holes as if to hide lightning storm raged above soaking curtain water they recognize passage another era given memorial circulations roots fallen green limbs budding new buds as if parody were culture wood fiber sap shade far distance telling shapes unknown now divine sounds transmitting atmosphere behind veil what might imagine larger context silence take presence the tree here one stands always in center feels tremor precession Axis trunk growth concordance species flourished cannot fathom use of course Law written device to mark delay actually defeat large whirling registers record in true future light ranged round with various ribbons strands laced threaded tendrils biome's filaments agglomeration named out of Earthfire strange peculiar discerning matter

Daughters at OKEANOS heard seen felt shift change all changes descendants from titanic parentage whose recent incarnation in form ZAS MOIRA resemble true relations to ancient pasts but nature of concealed essence in waves out of surge tides waters up down cave concealment this story over and over but this time archaic arch resonance has gone from hands on shafts emblematic Z in gold no longer gold turned white they launch toward land travel a cross-section re-entry exploding diplogenetic encapsulation of THERSEYN superimposed of ONÖNYXA as if on forefront atmosphere so day night become interanimations boundaries cross phenomenal bespeaking parentage Daughters in every story or tale told refabulates might of even despots rulers pass out this fodder this envelope news Faeries pantomime show perennial wish Daughters' projections toward longed for divinity dreams empire made also now interruption of those cycles embodied animation dividing two prime spheres of light Sun then Moon they step out dream humankind organismal genesis mineralization Daughters intersect THERSEYN reflect value water resource to carry future sea-caves springs which belt the waist of Earth out of archaic coalescings crossing boundaries the Law of Homo Sapiens

physical powers universe two born movement actual ascension phenomenal relationships light bodies water fire first Daughters out of OKEANOS brought to crossing THERSEYN ONÖNYXA elemental first lights in overlap all Daughters sign vehicle water brought to pool EKSTONISTIAN time planet observed Ovoid Mirror species drowning forgetfulness somehow Daughters brought to pool bathed understand at least witness vehicle water more important than air main sense water double-tailed snake THERSEYN's chest Daughters bathing also see silent movement his body coincide animation light form ONÖNYXA as if guardian protection snake in this bathers span water two wings upon transport emergence small distant joint articulation watery wings impregnate water world-pause shown acquisition of animation three kinds picture pose of animated presence transit fed much like plant nourished rainwater soil gives rise to roots nourishment returning phase brings essence world-pause visions eternal dreams of inter-animated phasing thru Daughters back to station at OKEANOS sense of hands work fingers on hands pointing labor shafts rods of which I've written so much depends upon pointing emblem adorns catapulted piece this age in world limited correspondence taken for granted atmosphere becomes clouded polluted Z-rods find way into land represent interpret Earth's time to ZAS his relation to MOIRA relation to PLNIPLOI big brain these fingers digits multiplied so exampled the individual ten seen flurry intense effort labor sight transportation ten into more than induces lost makes these memories emblematic Z ultimate representative to age stored potential memory used to further population ZAS rods shafts across into confirming land

Sons in front Ovoid Mirror saw living flight from incest out of water bathing how surface water caught fire ONÖNYXA began crossing double figure THERSEYN signal of singularity joined third element age almost entirely silent consumed psychology of song stick figure scratched in petrified petroglyph whereas third image attestation fire from water ONÖNYXA bears nearness to death not only symbolizes closeness nearness all things shows threat to lineage inheritance itself no matter flight from birth-site flight journey birth-site consummation flames nearness hiddenness ONÖNYXA revealed passage forgetfulness into memorialization her future THERSEYN's inhabitation her form elemental organismal embodiment all subsequent mito-embodiments

ONÖNYXA shown above Sons Daughters multiplication reflections light Mirror everyone enlarged middle reflects further nature out of forgetfulness physical embodiment but worth physical residing memorialized sense stands as crossroads node making Mansion of Night now repository light's making place vehicle time no longer theoretical by which humans project into universal reflective relay transit passages eras all ages here-to-fore unrecorded

between sun moon stars constellation THERSEYN ONÖNYXA divide into the following mansions each light source reflected multiple cluster watery flowing light matter sheathed shaded behind brighter surface fire carries expands consumes contracts light from center outward RORSHNAN KALAREEMABU NIXINITORI ZUKHIT YEEWOODAY KNEEKUN JNSAYHUN ORTHEBRAE LAY'NTEL GTAPHXIUCARTA POATÆYOESIS

milky night begins four corners parameters boxed-in species whose capabilities ever only intense pressure release while Ovoid Mirror controversy Sons Daughters pertains to viscera ONÖNYXA emptiness had content of contentions now full radiance udder ultimate negentropy seeks passage growth doubling size thru creation a belt out contiguous stars isolation flips toward least finds protean commensurability Meso-near voice once hollow transiting beyond prophetics

out of lightning division cells risen in center of the Bull a form of principle herd te dais upon which fiery star emanates dark patiently illuminates study concentration articulates now sight among transiting reflections illumination bloodlines desire radiance ever applicable beautiful reach satisfies warming ease inciting inspiration memory those who insist not sit lives outside the Ovoid Mirror ponder in void have no facility generating so of course lay Laws into void see hear Laws chatter incapacitation as if birds when even children know memories inside mothers birds interpret lay Laws map not in voids nor close-up strangling myopias shouts but reels of song stream's abundance charging head with coming birth correspondence pattern eternal seed still at work charging electrifying changing forms their present context

doubling made singly ongoing path time stoke emergencies crossing organismal fittings adaptations this passage then THERSEYN ONÖNYXA Ovoid Mirror's interior appendages vocabulary fitting slippage gestation plays out prolapse to come navel of the world histories into memories into dreams into hand once again matter or about to be one world shows limited apprehensions species outside mirror still a presence interior yet it is interior on exterior Mirror rumor controversy human everywhere unconsciously struggling Laws in contention rumor superstition habit dispelled or ingested long ago

ONÖNYXA pregnant two children THERSEYN acknowledged recognized further his more than faint trace any number of conceits entails human era growth in her sounding depth division advent belief beyond hearing Sons Daughters beyond visualization ONÖNYXA now biological bellowing sono-gram THERSEYN's seed embedded cycles surpass her own forgetting come upon memorialization true embodiment a sound light creature allowed transit Nightsky named every light intersection with THERSEYN a re-distribution of prioritization

Law defended attacked is it one side the Mirror only?

Sons a Daughters MOIRA now vilifies the very essence pregnancy progeny of ONÖNYXA saying *these children are not free this is why you have to see them for all intents and purposes Unborn of antagonism between sexes exists should be maintained there is to be order left at all otherwise that damned Mirror its Ovoid shape will consume everything no clearly outlined parameter to anything including Day Night the Pantheon itself will consume itself in its own reflective light every other symbolic instituting also fly off the ground to never return* so ZAS repeats to Sons the most ancient duality for persuasion so very convincing Sons Daughters prepare dig in for long materializing term

HOW THERSEYN part biological history while other embedded lightning the superstitious out of EKSTONISTIAN crossing underwent apotheosis spirit toward SHŌÖNWU into Erebus abused acknowledged recognized deep Earthly network Tartaros all the while Ovoid Mirror still contains travel back to Earth occupy Mansion of Night as if Nightsky resides in forgetfulness of ONÖNYXA a periodicity her psychic embodiment

*

* *

*

* * *

* *

* *

* *

* *

Children now angelic flight patterns near far citations Mirror thru Ovoid layerings theoretical distance in time space epochs equilibrations equations psychotic disturbances enlightening bios layers near close association decisive as well devicive illuminations transmissions hold release multiple forms wisdom higher unapproachable innocent appreciation temporal song SHIRU from EKSTONISTIAN primeval cord connecting OOM matrilineal continuation no simple adaptable panoplies appearance disappearance world increasingly divides as Mirror Ovoidal intimation among homo sapiens those who would remain

PLNIPLOI inheritance from ZAS brain drained to hold future incapacitation endure a way institute limitations consonant developments without twining sigil note allows swift vacuity seeming emanation from natural world rumor network echo voided development of the twins in utero waiting as well lurking as at the ready for slightest release of labor pause caesura appearance one after the other out of mother's immanence throes of dilating tissue and bone

how many buried bodies RED CIVILIZATIONS found now how many back to Earth unknown but birth of children reaches bones anatomies abandoned for this one chance mediate inter-animate features a limited very limited consciousness glows ability tracks stars deeper darkness this the essence forming ONÖNYXA two cells dreamspace lifetimes inter-animation emanating raw amniotic shared radiance OOM even as QAPTAKUSS went off into pretense now all these histories to ground within fluid carnality inside species' luminescence elucidation hiddenness essential mysteries harboring natures two as they corpus carry reflections

every new thing cannot reveal much more than place control place thought told to think place all roads meet this too never hears voices train of thought everything arranged by distant picture historical tableau frozen MOIRA supported by ZAS PLNIPLOI knows absolutely nothing of angelic realm only doxology in separation from twins cannot perceive distance outside newness the novelty aspect needs bypass far-off realities just what indexical features already added sentences pronouncements rolling halls walls pantheon judgment firm he cannot stand pictures museum pieces move or position impromptu sun-dial for instance distraction away from angle of shadows formation of light within quotidian quadrangles alerts chemistries disturbing entire congressional embodiment toward further investigation igniting realms of curiosity necessary appreciation morphologies time space co-incidence overlaps consummates previous assumption forms shapes stand might represent overall historical markings would induce futures out of pasts anthropological inheritance habits behaviors PLNIPLOI conducts not just blind screen ZAS puts physical phenomenal realms to create world deafness abuse verbal MOIRA since beginning her consolidation of power influence first won position symbolic representation species gave but morphed titanic qualities a monologue in dialogue plays ZAS procreativity actually an outgrowth verbosity told ZAS impregnate conceive PLNIPLOI comes exclusively thru commands into her appears apprehension of second twin resounds ONÖNYXA according to MOIRA so gone issuing belly either eaten shouted or other subjects clearly not merely conventional MOIRA's reach at best non-cyclical investment overlap immediacy neither thought nor need but desire for order yields her persuasive capacity

ONÖNYXA's belly radiation precessionary song SHIRU chords brought AHNÁHR back into non-dialectical light shows human attached itself to far near engine ambitions ultimate one over-riding seed egg neo-mechanical automatic self-regulation specter launch environments imagined or actual pictures utterances fantastical unleashes historical simplicities consonance of unknown mergers in this too moral ethical evolutions put to pasture grazing creation or destruction matter so incredibly sure within collective embodiment advent one device brought from union Earth's vast resource shows fulfillment toward denouement survival key building block universe admits thru matter once for all time astonishing soul-ridden contradictory stance outside the Mirror questions Ovoidal appearance as mere appearance amongst themselves doctrine of *entelechy dunamis* a framed potency to entrain masses fall lockstep harnessing deepening material fantasies of constructability

Sons Daughters outside the Mirror think no anatomy entered meanwhile ONÖNYXA in full Ovoidal daemonic gestational kind of dis-belief threatens existence bodies vehicles of homo sapientia embryos dancing into fetus dance every moment along arc from conception embodiment THERSEYN ONÖNYXA green inheritance EKSTONISTIAN at the same Ovoid Mirror dancing her belly jumping charge two the very passage from ignorance ignoring presence Mirror rehearsal one era lifetime examine near far become elements gravity of Earth discover primary step in crossing innards of the Mirror exuberance daemonicly coordination toward passage funneling winds so much part of THERSEYN's epoch era toward real tissues ONÖNYXA bounds eventually Earth connected to ONÖNYXA's acquisition passage memory from out her true embodiment cleansed creature devoid species historical verisimilitudes heading toward push vitalic currencies all of which correspond to THERSEYN never any other existence passes this world but thru birth canal realization children backward movement erases other backward glance here now twins prolapse essences into place entrance and exit both

F ar things commingle near both these non-understandable two lives one we tend say near at hand other far this finding focus with things aren't visual leads us believe the same have eye-sockets we say who or what about who what initiate who or what existence presence brought forth the same what is to explain notify incorporation body of bodies imparted to things to body land view to two overwhelming whelp bios living streams breaking bloody passages emergencies inter-breeding wild things inter-animation life giving spirit decays eaten by other living bios cycle essential distance of all distances a reality the human wefted warped by pull push animality then closer animations stages self-wracked guilt doubt terrors knowledge never tested til land rises into cranial capacity merges ghosts dreams potencies inter-penetrations spirits long dead spirits living specters out of architectures imaginations as well firm solid terra quality living shame abyss terrorizes to their insubordinate ground brings them closer

out of founderings humans recorded written contexts dug narrow crevice denies overlap passage issuing ONÖNYXA with future figures twins will reach those contexts not simply explore conquest maintenance of extinct empire nor uphold Faeries pantomime homo sapiens who think lift heavy objects yet undermine emanation activation far-flung near-sprung inter-capacitations presence presences of presence any and all markings lose direction no wonder the end they endure meanwhile the crown half-angel will find herself by dilation her own sensorium instantly refracting Law of light over above heads this miraculous vision channel connects all parts every anatomical discovery following diamond-like glints broken water splattered fallen ground as if furthest height OURANIAN THERSEYN's seems galvanize white light parameters of night house come to himself first time momentous preceding crowning cranium child he orders syllabification of lights ascendance Nightsky specifically house mansion marks ultimate crossing his return into Earth lights pointed furthest distinct light SHŌÖNWU tongue to quiver excitation length breadth name spindled unspooled farthest con-figures coincides calendar attends initializing cross electrical circuitry creates out of watery biotic features of THERSEYN

**FRĂʻAPLĒO**

in this tongue drawn point word eternal beyond temporal conclusions another child twin comes right on heels the first passage burns blood a fire spurting from ONÖNYXA the second head red tracings changed light morphed light series of flames manticized figurations her blood his crown t emerges into world sound of her stretching cries shooting corresponding atmosphere as if self could endure a species has no more to say saying in blood no self holds contains her own relation to the house at Earth returns sparks phenomenal world returns attempts mark or score day approximation element of groan deeply embodies boy twin to FRĂ'APLĒO

**ÉERȘAMON**

homo sapientia mad at this breach its own religious systems source-code Laws forever broken how is it two come from one evolutionary scandal rears itself now on back these children pushing rumors otherwise dominate horizon deep doubts deep questions begin within the species

second elucidation the first furthering consolidation passage so taken up by second in form of fire gotten from mother all the way back to OOM we see pantheon set relief waiting for this second forth not merely time the first a kind of measure but passage second slipped along to show ONÖNYXA out-of-body transcendence even from first moments here he is busy composing concentrated syllables mother's directions to plumb her unconscious depths feel out labor by her passage rime giving himself into time and space

essence the Fifth World brought to a close this simple paradigm one which human consciousness cannot contain by Laws Nations States nor even Stages of growth decay thinks institutions the pantheon PLNIPLOI coming of age first of the first one zero binary embodiment no match ultimately for sweeping crumbs off table groans a vast plain travelers civilizations all of it palm tossed atmosphere precessional to take simple motion sweep into hand up into air chronicler shows littlest the most forgotten will defeat slay actually decapitate capacity exegetes gigantic prophetic transposition the past into future present in presentation ONÖNYXA delivers the entire species into memory herself a passage of all passages slippages causes causeways in her smallness seed EKSTONISTIAN's THERSEYN completed every other perfect circle elongating precessionary passage an egg in shape Ovoid now gemstone un-Earthed plenipotentiary mineral reflection the heart of materiality Earth's hot core created

SHIRU begins his song feels new overwhelmed always to outlay chordal calling challenge withstand too easy try high low notes unbroken sense drew AHNÁHR beyond back into Earth to hear what thought seen twist turn in matter itself unborn light potency continuity entirely different trajectory inherent not simply force light synchronizes world least of light's concerns in the end humans fear they stand Sons Daughters a kind of mantra-like concentration brings same old trajectory to hang tribute ancestors in truth ancestors have or will thru Mirror any day now crowded out light air thick figures opacity blocked ability see hear evolution the first distinguishing feature species biotic realm somehow fulfilling destiny rocks minerals caves Daughters tracks Sons made thru desert in search the RED CIVILIZATIONS connection to time space to ZAS subservient figure to MOIRA those two alone lead all back to pantheon restore valorize validate beings their livelihoods minerology planet undergoing tremendous re-alignment essentiality in funneling winds a kind of theogony of THERSEYN whereby marrow bones in template of anatomy mankind erodes re-nutritioned a martial benediction soul-seed blood gives soil tissues cells enlarges consigns persuasion of light out of darkness a kind of balm soothing caress time turns animal natures human opacity non-transmissive non-transitory while pantheon an ever-ready exposition for various traits the species more bearing mineral exhalation inhalation thru caves at OKEANOS as well Tartaros split into upper as well sucking lowering drafts no one attempts but some leap enters one way or another

place much more powerful than any this vast plain upon which children deposit in a twinned variation mother's father's whereabouts continually re-arriving fact THERSEYN into dynamism ONÖNYXA brings attachments singularly together so future spells nearness as well depth their farther biotic apprehending selves base apprehensions those two seed egg change take variation descent unquestionably this place upon which house parameters Earth beginning water and fire

Sons attempt another big move Mirror show progress land a value above beyond present advent so e-vent really somewhat eclipses adheres thinks to sweat so much muscles in stark relief to mntns perspective seems little progress but up close little muscle huge quality fine art but massive frame they burden cannot put up little jabs artistic renderings efforts because quickly fails the scale shifts size weight Mirror cycle of rumors begins murmur within Mirror appears at distant horizon once again a kind of entrapment oversees now a faint but clear sharp note SHIRU by Sons as if echo of much desired freedom

ÉERȘAMON the last blessing out from ONÖNYXA's egg human pure shape sends out sound echo first mouthings verbalizations twins echoic ringing series ringlets Ovoidal shape wobbles into realm EKSTONISTIAN's legend two are apo-theotic relationship to human history their shape bypasses prophetic Fifth World whose projected middle ground a stage in development species at one lowly end mis-management absolute corruption of speech in form OÖND's double QAPTAKUSS whose adobe City of Holes into rebellion then later inhabitants dead mysteriously murdered remains un-Earthed paleoanthropologists archeologists clues to disappearance gives rise wild speculations slow sifting accumulating evidence on the other the upshot trajectory here in Ovoidal rings ringlets sound making way EKSTONISTIAN's constellation never had receptivity in pantheon except thru force of her own hiddenness revealed herself then of course the final revealing thru AHNÁHR's penetration formation of THERSEYN by that same pool now ÉERȘAMON lay in post fetal expressionism flowering eventuality **FRĂ'APLĒO** to become food for angelic exegesis most distant times places she the first to emerge out of ONÖNYXA the full crossing into THERSEYN shows essential astronomical personal particularity physical martiality SHŌÖNWU precessional lights the shell Tortoise Earth's atmospheric curve Snake with two tails THERSEYN descended purely physical relationship stars days times back into Earth to set within containment the Mansion of Night ZAS left behind this new age inside night flames rushed up out the pool EKSTONISTIAN THERSEYN's empirical opinions of nature Faerys gabbed about for aeons snake realized embodiment fire out of water the primal syzygy now attends Ovoidal waves sound making way into first born's capacity for human sight angelic embryonic vision

Daughters understand absolute material necessity their we-avings catapultation ejaculations out of OKEANOS into convergence of Earth a reproductive round not only in time but good number now simply let go with next cycle of emblematic rods they enter Ovoidal Mirror kinetics of their own labor lands them within martial aspect SHŌÖNWU into realms of Erebus-issue as well funneling winds Axis-Tree aspects nature of light within without any and all constellations

SHIRU knows importance of ÉERȘAMON's birth **FRĂ'APLĒO**'s birth sings and in song once again erecting whereby return AHNÁHR into Earth coincides direction within bodies human species potentiality so smaller access EKSTONISTIAN here ÉERȘAMON aroused SHIRU once again establishes on air State by which living things might see themselves so it was AHNÁHR the first correspondence regardless of what written spoken before his turn-around back into atmosphere this embodiment accomplished too signal moment species makes toward song SHIRU to set penetrating view of previously apprehended distances time space SHIRU silenced or when brought into silence also discharges anthropomorphic to accomplish new pregnancy for world in semblance of human re-creation Anthropos until he takes song again forgetting re-enters sensorium traits passed in neither physical isolation nor absolute worship of representation a kind of pure void emptiness human mind might comprehend characteristics carry generation formation future past non-calculative non-biological destinies embodiment of the passage like Ovoidal Mirror trait neither one Law physics nor Law astronomy to come perfect rest in knowledge secure usability the Mirror's portal isn't simply matter attaining time or calendrical association by which might spurt action it is property light even tho science understands speeding element capture speed part of its essence this why PLNIPLOI at the brink of great discovery against his own brain about to apply the world at large anything outside himself but at last performs complete network flatline sends brain's signal into all existent allies in rumor hearsay inoculates with sleep his entire capacity signal led to believe totality of being as well exact opposite totality in other words what doesn't exist but THERSEYN opposed still opposes PLNIPLOI did not succumb why he crossed supernal toward SHŌÖNWU re-martialed being back to cross essence with ONÖNYXA

Sons working movement the Mirror see alignment sun moon follow related verticality to track cross land so in this verticality begins pantheon separates out as thing or object every content in vertical substitution any other anywhere four corners so this geo-political their collective as opposed to geo-graphic reason they position Earth an adamant refusal recognize anything outside parameters vertical reality horizontal movement their workings laborings some not just into Mirror to find what the other side might tell but other directions steppings away from discovered Mirror wasn't necessarily where Sons say it is!

SHIRU manifests song timeless spell undoing potential for acquiescence extinction species marks stasis no longer in thrall to their various quandaries ONÖNYXA sleeps as twins fool around the pool of EKSTONISTIAN world they see hear Faerys Forest scenes conscious attributes mirror back light they suck sustenance in the future passages from birth toward death decay or death demise beginnings of life Faerys inter-staging projections both animate inanimate **FRĂ'APLĒO** and ÉERȘAMON take note silly figurations laugh at antics faces to portray the true scale of powers all systems knowing all networks including PLNIPLOI's twins at this early date pantheon how it circulates to shake out various relativities in a way they always return dense copse these elemental shenanigans stone wood dirt water will need SHIRU sings out the entire air's anatomy Faerys enstage anatomies a primal feast isolated from human species there is strength small chinks light insect-ual world atomizes to what time re-constitutes condensed inter-availability first instauration what remaining wilderness

Mansion of Night THERSEYN not exactly forms death nonetheless forms activations re-birth re-entry partial so Daughters at OKEANOS have known to be entranced so fevered emblem upon staff the rod the we-ave itself catapults from caves sent so far into atmosphere penetrates beyond atmosphere and in those heroic flights channeling every spirit ever known conceived reincarnation karmic wheeling literal material space outside atmosphere of ZAS the re-entered Earth of AHNÁHR this furthest farthest declension of all absolutes a feature the species glimpses furthest farthest appears accounts a trackless maze the fullest void not emptied this goes contrary to Law does re-define Law begins cycling vast reaches cannot go far enough Daughters teach by this principle unbeknownst to them statutes re-interpreted set up re-interpretation doesn't matter what specific catapultation seems time to re-code involute turn Earth cycles calendrical associations make way ZAS MOIRA pantheon entire rumoring alternate to start all over again

celestial events b wield focus back Earth world in change advent unleashed from time hunting anything errant brought species sniff out of hiding to move Mirror from piece of land but matter itself entire difficulty as if homo sapiens left to their own no other guide scale things out of whack space itself impossible it why adaptations biological facets of homo such now position ONÖNYXA did why THERSEYN crossing destination his lifetime into death seemed end retrieves archeo-typical r of beings further brings ONÖNYXA recapitulation in some respects taboo incestualization re-married prospect to EKSTONISTIAN finally ascertained it was this realization stars positions realize night was home so ONÖNYXA would shelter twins raise conjunction coordination to endlessness starry depths to coordination pantheistic maneauvers eyes ears a way into out of House or Mirror sometimes a double for the other but so strictly strung network to start again end again distant nearness atmosphere something heard

ONÖNYXA waking beginning life beginning she knows passes thru so she to no responsibility except first the species enables reach toward nothing but procreative impulse dynamic identity finally all stories tossed out but one

signal flashes night air containment parameters **FRĂ'APLĒO** to hunger in light of angelic nature touches both mortal as well immortal wave gem-like crystallization reflections born new world no longer absolute rush toward MOIRA might call center the House a kind of re-ordering re-alignment historically correct model whereby all abeyance even ZAS phenomenal world her own seat this night now sluicing forward child's hunger in form of first water made spirits out of Erebus shadows mineralizations circulating thru World-Tree by way of OKEANOS Daughters now souls toward SHŌÖNWU met concordance this night because stalled but the chest of THERSEYN burning re-entry into atmosphere it was for ÉERȘAMON the second born will always be that way one two first second in the night lights scinitillant hints of fire out of history THERSEYN became by act re-entry father even as he did not know even too MOIRA blotted everything out her position maintains pretend pose recall animation out of marble out of form ZAS created as he touched but philanderer wanting touch everything why MOIRA constantly keeps tabs on ZAS otherwise he'd off into new age sleep the first doorway entrance he came to

PLNIPLOI responds to stimulation the world goes into routine his brain to drive entrance the world away in signal his own cortical radiates Sons Daughters who up til now heard PLNIPLOI thru urgencies of MOIRA so their fingers speed work know PLNIPLOI as child not presence the future but who in fact point posture MOIRA ZAS now this new world PLNIPLOI corresponds to futures hidden he is behind the present modality histories why MOIRA goads ZAS arrive at PLNIPLOI's room show the world picture over and over ZAS involved with something really no desire anymore embodiment of MOIRA now PLNIPLOI keeps in obedience duty to summon loosely organized vaguely known phenomenality so at back his head gaping holes sights easily filled Daughters each of which thinks to take from work query their thoughts upon Z-rod catapultations routinely perform and in temptation both Daughter and ZAS arise conductivity announces vision work in form singular Daughter MOIRA grows angered ZAS begun differently organized spell or rumor but of course all she can do is wait for ZAS materialize so flies into consolidation speaks to fact of insubordination *ZAS dear you need to understand time your responsibility arrived your own posture sit up don't slouch take your body walk let me see how you look passing thru the pantheon without interruption can you do this for me just this once?*

cosmogonic ONÖNYXA such the twins now up on her those magnificent breasts light itself delights new forms sap milch pap **FRĂ'APLĒO** into realms of light down little ventricles dilated feeling ONÖNYXA supplies the little girl sucking furiously tenderized nipples the difference in this age non-existent light powerful light itself causing **FRĂ'APLĒO** to blind early eyes with feeling nipple cause to every future reflection future surface orientation presents no history comparable to surface apprehension these sweet lips sweet nipple fundament to all moving flowing matter

MOIRA sees twins on ONÖNYXA's breasts but divorced from scene not sure they pose no movement animation nothing but pose brings shadowy essence searches correct pose needs find comparison of poses can she get another version PLNIPLOI to mimic her breasts have two not one child would she do with two eyes cloud ZAS as if all his fault his nature how it ranges entirety of OURANIA sniffing another duplicity has got to stop she can't take it anymore forces skin become marbleized more than ever holding breath in the hallway the pantheon once again attained proper dimension complete realization opinion all glory this age epoch ascending right side the pantheon no longer muddled overlap no longer confused by any breast pap

little ÉERȘAMON turning closeness inside out begins sputter lips tongue purling delight entrance the nipple good gurgle gush of milk into his mouth and throat

here comes now spitting fire Earthly nexus matter crossed by double-tailed Snake THERSEYN sexualized crossing borne ONÖNYXA out of ÉERȘAMON's little mouth lips emerge multiple eyes heads snake flames out multiple tongues beside **FRĂ'APLĒO** whose inheritance of ONÖNYXA's gone capacity marks her new-born consciousness eternity two given sight toward ground ONÖNYXA's body become invisible shrine of space center-pole World-Tree begins emanate THERSEYN's presence fully descended to place her sheltering invisible body now no more mortal bearing her place apotheosis summoning stars night of ZAS come down to mortality human frame once again not thru agony nor projected indifference of picture perfection nor good but exigency THERSEYN incalculable substance synonymous matter her spirit shot thru out Tartaros wisped into Ovoid Mirror overlap of **FRĂ'APLĒO** can see flowing vocabulary infant eyes now circulations of ascending souls both in the world heading out toward precessionary activations the planet wrinkles scintillations of light specter of her mother traveling thru Mirror into funneling winds toward parameters of night show inside x-rayed spectral dimension sight a kind of sigh from inhabitants within Mirror collectively realize disappearance invisibility mortal ONÖNYXA her passage the eye by way of angelic infant **FRĂ'APLĒO** whose fire-tongued brother continues feeding frenzy delights at the breast of ONÖNYXA

AHNÁHR now visits ZAS dimensions tricky but converses all the while MOIRA speeding cross dimension time and space to head AHNÁHR off does so with trepidation really doesn't want to deal with the era AHNÁHR initiates one of lightning the right amount of energy built inside ZAS explosions felt thru-out the entire fabric contentiousness has to be dealt with carefully decides watch conversation from a distance turns herself to one of ZAS's many cloudy accumulations of vapor as AHNÁHR speaks *if this persuasion took place in another time and place you might be able ZAS continue unification of all presence or rather I mean MOIRA could but it's not possible any longer to remain married to what is essentially an urgent factor alone the very nature of the kosmos opened itself up to humans they have no need of the pantheon or should I say no need to her version of the kosmos this why Law re-written even when and where you think it isn't*

naked sun-charts syllables unleashed ÉERȘAMON THERSEYN he feels corresponding disappearance ONÖNYXA rock his being a kind of sadness ecstatic release circulates thru the planet now on tongue ÉERȘAMON oracular exposition the soul of ONÖNYXA embarks to tell time emerging adherents inhabitants one consciousness stored another in the exterior and by effort attains the present age just as fire comes from milk essentiality flows into watery cross-fertilization inherent **FRĂ'APLĒO**'s infant exploratory heart mind visualization now various angles Platonic Solids once again another whose accidence no accidence ÉERȘAMON sputters new language neo-geometric recapitulation of space bones might have been RED

CIVILIZATIONS shudder planetary rocking ground under THERSEYN's feet he witnesses Snake tails turn Snake heads sparkling obsidian reflections above a flickering bifurcated tongue lapping at the edge of felt atmospherics

two energies two propensities for light enter confluence occurs stirring elemental **FRĂ'APLĒO** contacts memorialization her mother neither held in mind nor embrace at the breast THERSEYN inter-sections all things in sacral deposit her eyes merge into one summons animation the world resembles SHŌÖNWU by ability to transport transit transparent spaces Night as well ONÖNYXA makes way thru circulations Earth's abundant riches in this way **FRĂ'APLĒO** sees the pantheon in new unfolding evolutionary aspect where force-field of power plays ad infinitum into out of aspiration vain noble alike fly center-beam visual power one with SHŌÖNWU prepares souls by THERSEYN translates celestial regions magnetic pull manifested morphologies of Tortoise Snake animalian transfer homo sapiens toward insistence on war procreative act cellular structures aberrantly anatomical THERSEYN collage assemblage these creatures stand for Light constellations eras will pass again but exception exists persistence polar magnetic accumulation understandings observations Axis-Tree wobbling rotating pleasureful activity out of El Niño into La Niña THERSEYN sees heard lone capacity ONÖNYXA so turns as if thru center **FRĂ'APLĒO** too enlivens hot-spot third eye ganglia anatomy of man she sees not only mother wending upward Axis-Tree's umbrella ejaculating l renditions of sight holds capacitation transits correspondence takes on semblance of such vision

urgency in the world wraps itself round rumors circulates suspends Mirror in middle the land as if completed tool for enlightenment something a-voided at all costs reflections coalescing into one reflection as if Sons cannot move Ovoid Mirror Daughters cannot approach from their stronghold at OKEANOS not so much work anymore but abandonment so all renditions of sight in human realm now under suspicion reason alone works consonant rising sun brief appearance moon nightlight on table-top Sons think about path entrenched soil how this attracts verticality rumors of horizontal activities swirl meanwhile brains of Sons so involved of the Mirror cannot approach but by envisioning projection their own work isolates other features exist in the world even imaginary worlds so MOIRA now understands connexion between PLNIPLOI his absolute potency and Sons unifying force the future become adamantly obvious a moment of immanence and thus moments of the clock and time again the entire pantheon phenomenal world radiating tiny inexistent apparition planted in cortical manifestation of the present order of elements directions the entire celestial inhabited pantheon radiates to first fire now comes from young ÉERȘAMON then syllables tongues a net of sight reflection far into future **FRĂ'APLĒO** has very first attribute ability to see sight itself then below tawny Earth distant blue light blue atmosphere element of water and air ONÖNYXA transparency all things we breathe understand apogee perigee inhalations exhalations tie-ins to ecstasy extinction species so there she goes now down crevasse Earth the final direction from place where THERSEYN was ridiculed abyss taken congregation of shadows in Erebus ONÖNYXA persists clears out sounds begin again the Mirror talked about by some walked into by others

watery reflections travel **FRĂ'APLĒO** as she divines absolute distance all distances take THERSEYN into her dimension as growth assumes changes calendricizes accordingly so in one age view such acknowledged force held in one something else again when released from hold into acquisition recognition new or un-told forces chime charm **FRĂ'APLĒO** as water gem-like radiance stone whose transposition to Nightsky effectual as that upon Earth intersection two governances accord planetary magnetics precessionary activity of time itself 26,000 year recapitulation of true north but diadem the eye now tears up wells up the very being **FRĂ'APLĒO** not a philosophy out the pantheon but re-organization of approach to matter by way of lifetime a seer reflector taken to mean THERSEYN seed too within outward crystallization force watering turn magnetics of Earth seat toward vision weeps now life's full capacity not so much relation to geo-desic properties of family nor transparency ONÖNYXA who has taken circulations of shadows elementals she knows distance between things impossible true complete self-reflection manifests will always travel multi-dimensional sensory tympanums the heart palpable tools of perception transpositioned symbolic register to change portals magnetics mortality an errant free dimension discovery itself not as thing but stony silence within spirit ancestral anatomy formed

everything at one time ZAS intuits why he shows fundament all ages but not simply representative function to be part of age he is that created his own movement toward Daughters sew emblems with great adherence onto spindle shaft as it is ready for catapultation whence movements lights over horizon seen heard the shaft the rod Z prominent gold Daughters translating OKEANOS into land out of water into dirt always this motion a few recognize holds creation while others repulse to connect telepathically RED CIVILIZATIONS signal differences between right wrong they go to trance bypass essence ZAS so too bypass consort MOIRA adjust eyes bodies attitudes pose position righteousness gleaned from differentiations in things categorized as bad some good eventually meted this the reason MOIRA into form of future like

ONÖNYXA like EKSTONISTIAN to come out infant son PLNIPLOI might retain the nature of creation a nascent self into work the posers re-align signal within network PLNIPLOI employs entire Kosmos somehow even if only brief spell holding PLNIPLOI re-ordering creation gold ZAS coordination Daughters at OKEANOS sense ZAS's role subsumed by the fact creation makes MOIRA worried cataleptic creature urgencies mirror catapultations ZAS rods in this she is taken out of the pantheon as if some self-comportment attributed to EKSTONISTIAN's presence in the world finally at this late date we see MOIRA making way to the most hidden Forest at last seeking face-to-face knowledge of this woman who changes shape not in usual morphologies skin bone but retreat surge blood founding into out of signals above beyond the pantheon even MOIRA's own merge forces creation itself in gestation and birth of PLNIPLOI

ÉERȘAMON provides a depth of space Daughters provide ZAS elucidation representation his existence thru-out the phenomenal relation to **FRĂ'APLĒO** not escaped ZAS nor MOIRA the signal reason for change in direction they head into emanations source-code will release into present by which everything conjured worked upon Sons too in verticality their work cannot see a desert in any direction in fact four directions given way to eight by virtue the Mirror shows their own horizons Ovoid in shape no matter how they appeal to Law or historical development dissolution RED CIVILIZATIONS just this kind of approach SEVLESMEHT saw he accepted inverted nature jumped into his own mantic fire swallowing seed-spark flames self-ascension at first marked by one star RORZHNAN the fire which at first circulated stream of Nightsky overlap at OKEANOS and as he knew Daughters lept into fire outgrowth milky flow light so apprehending made contact AVISTAVARZERVAIRYU great goddess constellation overlap to the pantheon this kind of rumor released horizon of the world by virtue of sun's light each and every day creation centers living souls at first inhabitants of Earth then moves organizations becomes so hot even water which was only balm in common flames reaches into networked connexion humans animals biotic catch fire from source creation this the birth **FRĂ'APLĒO** sees begins toward flight within tissues bones sinews joints crackle spit-up echo from ÉERȘAMON her brother guardian

OÖND now roleplays transmissive light for ONÖNYXA questioning entire land round new eyes opens tandem event inaugurated disappearance of THERSEYN ONÖNYXA reappears OÖND's final pronouncement? Earth captivates mankind the final words spoken here OÖND rids himself every vestige of the past QAPTAKUSS his other whose many eyes not the ones we see today sad eyes looked upon ONÖNYXA left once again this time no anger nothing to rally in rearguard or seek with capabilities gone her charge the story every forgetting become mother OOM herself yet nor missing this overlap continuance could not before the fall of QAPTAKUSS new issues pass rumoring world representations in phenomenal all seemingly lost at first but offspring ONÖNYXA took THERSEYN complete utter pathos his own turn mirrors OÖND mirrors activation symbolically unused past returns to be his last utterance nothing his mouth not even breath passing out of himself into another world trans-intimacy phenomenal boundaries association ken into past QAPTAKUSS sought raise an entire civilization by images of denotation based on scurry of human eyes in groove or track a maze tho never solved one ear to other on and on every distance yield his panopticonic familiarity as if prophecy of forgetting were what she drew out of that terror ONÖNYXA took animal spirit lept the unused portion the human QAPTAKUSS's hold to find most iconic phallic representation enshrined snatched it for darkness welling the entire race saving by initiating forgetful zone where night now wakes over land

**FRĂ'APLĒO** knows light which came to eyes ONÖNYXA confluence unexpected disappearances event made civilization of QAPTAKUSS part ways what held its hold OÖND so two eyes now release tracking human head extinction of the species complete fumes memory long enforced rule QAPTAKUSS whose City of Holes controlled lands as far as horizons multiplied OÖND surveys two eyes feels presence of twins constellations two mysterious figures come full embodiment event forever now erasing occluding recognition distant uncultivated sentience part legacy this figure from implanted figures a racetrack from ear to ear symbolic goad unknowing unacknowledged out of SHIRU ringing atmosphere consonant every other event released recognition from historical purpose evokes represents half the souls but Mirror Ovoid shape takes relationship of thing seen to thing passed Erebus issues stars in passage of light dark underground planetary core fires out of Tartaros rounds ellipses passing news atmosphere mankind has run out of time

except shared portion clay dirt minerality from beginning traverses Ovoid Mirror Sons out of distant forgotten obliterated past works up sweat dis-cozzened undiscovered hopeful bodies float given one break in flow come understand future sucking winds out of SHŌÖNWU but this loss they most fear movement cannot connote and mirror shines a second in lapse but quicker stronger able-bodied more willing to pick Mirror move show progress the Ovoid shape now a carrot bag of oats on a horse buggy shows historical live-action capture once again cinema effort the moment a return to work yields and yields never invisible but this side the human species cannot be concerned with invisible behind Ovoid lantern they quash with muscular availability un-used for any break penetration of aether never coordination of Platonic Solids immersed in Mirror's shape consonant to door an entrance the next world PLNIPLOI already made resemble not the future but pantheon in his one concentrated signal bears to QAPTAKUSS but he is Buddha of afterlife regressions while Ovoid shape lingers in the world a form among forms not yet wasted in cycles of ZAS's legacy

language now from Sons into Daughters relay base to figure the entire potency of all communication locking guarantees and nothing else nothing the phenomenal to question by variant view all held in channel of work signal all languages a detonation of post-symbolic realization to re-instate the world

## sketches, *the nature of*]

"Experience can never experience the beginning immediately but also cannot attain it through any dialectics."

H., *The Event*

**no hinge to a body ens creatum** but hinge opens to a multitude of limbs off the centrality of time and space as in allegory : ἄλλος which is a differentiation or distance to the sighted realm what might be "other" correspondent consonance a version of presence

and ἀγορεύω an aggregation of speech related thru *agora* we now see as lens refracting relationships thru commerce so our distortion of speech makes commodified packaged delivery of selves instead of units of speech however that may be the

unity of allegory a ceasing of consonance as some sort of forwarding of the nature of what is being spoken *about* but is also a way backward in space and time and from that backwards motion we have the sense that what rumor formed presence most moved all these people in the very beginning of THERSEYN no hinge to any *one* body

and in that beginning he does not alone correspond to any one person or relation or set of relations but to one figure of the human

HE

embodied disembodied alike enacts the absolute birth of the tongue out of lightning charge that catapulted EKSTONISTIAN into the stars as well as and at the same time created canopy of her hiding in the forested world and in this green world was allowed to contract

the smallest size of her being to let fear and hunting nature the human the predatory pass over so too shots of light and electrical perturbations trebled into the skull of THERSEYN involuted source smallest pebble found in vase of a house plant for instance

well then you ask what does this have to do with the poem the emergence of ONÖNYXA out of the poem as a presence of the daughter who thefted symbol of power in order to enact the originary source EKSTONISTIAN?

the answer lies in her beginning to realize correspondence to THERSEYN their births from the very same source make-believe plain in the ordaining of them at the foot of the base of the totem of what *was* power OÖND giving to them both the return to this world thru such dual means unacknowledged by human history

returning ability to appear together anywhere any time only because both exist in the larger presence of OOM mother genetrix of story's charge the hidden consort of humanity

this understanding duality was *his* source ("power") even corrupted thru rumor ONÖNYXA's nature stole for her own gratification realizes is and was limited visualization their understanding application the new order Earth OOM corresponds to EKSTONISTIAN the same albeit not the hunted now but from an era has passed on to the past they can be twinned by the same correspondence dismissing separate "roles" for one history plays "unconditionally" (they being removed from real experience)

now brought for review the return of ONÖNYXA and at this moment she sees THERSEYN by her side receiving strokes from the symbol of OÖND

HE just as soon disappears to HER in this activity disappearance of his corporeality shows true power the symbolic always granted motion from OÖND as a goal of all any ever wanted

OOM the plantation of that magic by which ONÖNYXA could only understand in reaching to steal touch symbol and charge it move symbol into her encounter with parameters of Earth-space while HE filled incorporeality the same unnoticed so takes on the name Spirit a switch-a-roo

ONÖNYXA discovered

true turning of allegory her own experience of timespace in stars the furthest reaches the complications of recorded time as it meets sidereal confusions in time so that forward backward become confused and the tally of herself as metaphoric Sophia ceases to be anything but a name spawned from simple cloaking one *thing* for another *thing*     forgetfulness led to the limpness of Law under symbols of power her father OÖND had fallen in lock-step with

HER

nature hungered and in that hunger the gathering of speech into a logic pronounced itself as illogical so the world of spoken things always waiting for her to re-make that self     viable desire     clearing for free vocalization comes from one desire to steal OÖND's *unused* power ever she of course "owns"

under which power EKSTONISTIAN becomes fugitive     living enactment of the self-ordained moment of expansion as well as contraction never to contradict her dictation from a completely unannounced figure     a totem capable of all correspondence in a magical realm     EKSTONISTIAN     understanding time as neither one correspondence nor another     freely accepting filaments over a long period of time in hiding     created THERSEYN from the pool which formed her most secret place     Earth in a verticality     creation out of which incubation THERSEYN as lover and child formed form the *only* correspondent to Spirit     HER too     not single and solitary not captive to symbolic meaning her flight into secret canopied green hiddenness knows the elemental trunk all signs ultimately intersect

****
***
**
*

Out the great evolution of projection
Paths meet intertwine
intimate
relations
None greater than drive to EKSTONISTIAN's abode

From which the endless pool
surfaces occasions Earth itself
Abyss out of which THERSEYN's skull
Electrified tongue in her midriff
dug out earliest artefact
Shards of energy whose view postulates limbs
umbilically derived
Incomparable unique attending
approach then touch
felt by AHNÁHR first as song
Bursts thru her SHIRU's call
essence limnal significance
Brought underworld roots of a storied tree
commencing sockets into formation
Disturbs shakes off surface from depth
shows what seeing sees
Along historical plexus breathing raw soundtime

**T THILLEMAN** is the author of 30 books of poetry and prose, including *Three Sea Monsters (Our History of Whose Image)* in which journal entries and poetic sequences investigate the legacy of Pound's redactions to Fenollosa's original manuscript version of *The Chinese Written Character as a Medium for Poetry*; *Snailhorn (fragments)*, a 360 poem cycle utilizing vedic transitions in celestial to allegorical articulation; and a novel *Gowanus Canal, Hans Knudsen*. His literary essay/memoir, *Blasted Tower*, was issued by Shakespeare & Co./Toad Suck in 2013. *The Special Body*, a second work of literary comment is available from Rain Mountain Press. A third booklength essay entitled *Image/Event* is forthcoming, as well as further Sketches. tt's pastel drawings and readings are archived at conchwoman.com.

www.ingramcontent.com/pod-product-compliance
Lightning Source LLC
Chambersburg PA
CBHW080636170426
43200CB00015B/2863
* 9 7 8 1 9 4 1 1 9 6 8 0 9 *